The Pocket Encyclopedia of World Aircraft in Color
FIGHTERS IN SERVICE
ATTACK AND TRAINING AIRCRAFT
SINCE 1960

The Pocket Encyclopedia
of World Aircraft in Color

FIGHTERS IN SERVICE

ATTACK AND TRAINING AIRCRAFT
SINCE 1960

by
KENNETH MUNSON

Illustrated by
JOHN W. WOOD

Frank Friend
Brian Hiley
William Hobson
Tony Mitchell
Jack Pelling

Revised Edition

Macmillan Publishing Co., Inc.
New York

Copyright © 1971, 1975 by Blandford Press Ltd.

All rights reserved. No part of this book may be reproduced or transmitted in any form or by any means, electronic or mechanical, including photocopying, recording or by any information storage and retrieval system, without permission in writing from the Publisher.

Macmillan Publishing Co., Inc.
866 Third Avenue, New York, N.Y. 10022

Library of Congress Cataloging in Publication Data

Munson, Kenneth G
  Fighters in service.
  (The Pocket encyclopedia of world aircraft in color)
  First published in 1966 under title: Fighters: attack and training aircraft, now greatly revised and expanded.
  1. Fighter planes. I. Title.
UG1242. F5M86   1975   358.4'3   75-12742
ISBN 0-02-587960-X

The original volume *Fighters, Attack and Training Aircraft*
first published 1966 (reprinted 1967)
First American Revised Edition 1975

Color printed by The Ysel Press, Deventer, Holland
Text printed and books bound by Richard Clay (The Chaucer Press) Ltd.,
Bungay, Suffolk, England

PREFACE

When the original two volumes in this 'Pocket Encyclopaedia' were published in 1966 they were regarded as something of an experiment, and included the major aircraft types then in service, regardless of age. In the years which have followed, the original idea has given rise to a whole series of volumes to cover the major civil as well as military aircraft of the world, from the Wright *Flyer* onwards, each volume covering a convenient period of time.

When the original two titles were first revised in 1971, it seemed appropriate to amend them completely to cover the period from 1960 onwards, discarding earlier aircraft which would then appear in other volumes covering the period 1945-60. The effect of this was to permit the inclusion of a greater variety of contemporary aircraft so that some three-quarters of the new volume consisted of new or extensively-revised material. This policy has continued in the present edition, in which the number of basic types included has been increased from 80 to 89.

As usual, thanks are again due to Ian D. Huntley for his continuing advice on the matter of colours and markings. Other kind friends who made material available or offered help in other ways included, particularly, Marcelo W. Miranda and John W. R. Taylor; to them also my thanks are extended.

October 1974

INTRODUCTION

In recent years it has become increasingly difficult to continue to classify military aeroplanes by such simple and straightforward descriptions as fighter, attack aircraft or trainer. Up to the time of World War 2 such classifications were still relatively clear-cut. A fighter was an aeroplane which went up into the air to engage other aeroplanes; a bomber was designed specifically to drop bombs; a fighter with the added ability to carry a few small bombs externally was a fighter-bomber; and trainers existed purely to provide flying or specialised duty training.

By contrast, today there are no such clear-cut distinctions. There is instead a multiplicity of tactical and strategic roles which military aircraft must play, each designed to fit into a particular niche in an integrated system of defence or attack. There are point-defence interceptors, air superiority fighters, day and all-weather fighters; close support, ground attack and strike aircraft; and practically every jet basic trainer in existence is employed, or can be employed, in a secondary role for attack. The margins of distinction between most of these categories grow ever more indistinct, for today we are in the midst of an age of multi-mission combat aircraft, able to turn their hand with equal ease to low-level attack or high-level interception, often at two or more times the speed of sound. One of the latest examples of this trend, under development by Great Britain, Germany and Italy for service in the latter half of the 1970s, has indeed been known for many years simply as the MRCA or Multi-Role Combat Aircraft.

Thus has the present pattern emerged and developed since the beginning of the 1960s. Nevertheless, the basic functions of the 'pure' fighter, if such a creature still exists, remain valid. The roles of such an aircraft are to provide defence for its own bases against attack, and to establish and maintain control of the air for advanced surface-based elements of its own forces. All that has basically changed, in a process that began in the mid-1950s, is the way in which the jobs are done.

Reference was made in the previous edition of this book to the decline in the use, so far as fighters were concerned, of the permanently-installed gun as the primary weapon. In the interception role at least, the function of the shell-firing gun was, for a decade or more, ousted almost entirely by the air-to-air missile, guided either by infra-red homing devices or by radar to strike down an enemy that the pilot who fires it never sees. Now the built-in gun is again regarded as an essential requirement in any modern fighter. The advent of stand-off weapons posed a threat against which the 'local' fighter, able to patrol only a few hundred miles from a fixed base, could not provide a one hundred per cent defence – and in a nuclear weapon age nothing less than one hundred per cent can be considered acceptable. So there arose larger and more complex fighters, able if necessary to patrol for long periods, with the aid of in-flight refuelling, packed with advanced, computerised navigation/attack systems for locating and intercepting an opponent in all weathers and with other equipment enabling them to avoid or counter the jamming or misleading of these systems by the enemy.

By the mid-1960s, such excellent Western types of interceptor as the Convair F-106, BAC Lightning and Dassault Mirage III could be counted superior in sophistication and performance to contemporary Soviet designs. The balance of power, however, is one which never remains static, and by the early 1970s the balance of fighter power was much less inclined in favour of the Western nations. America, having been faced with the mounting débâcle of the sorry F-111 saga, and having passed over the outstanding Lockheed YF-12 as a Mach 3 high-altitude fighter, was only at the design/development stage with its two latest fighter types, the carrier-based swing-wing Grumman F-14 Tomcat and the U.S.A.F's fixed-wing McDonnell Douglas F-15 Eagle. These were designed for a Mach 2·5 performance and for service introduction in the mid-1970s, yet on current estimates they are no more than equal to Russia's Mach 3 Foxbat fighter, which was designed in the early 1960s and has been in service for several years. The Foxbat's 1965 and 1967 world records gave a strong indication of its basic performance capabilities, and it re-emphasised them in 1973 with yet more record achievements. There can be nothing but cold comfort for the West in the knowledge that this aircraft was operational long before either the Tomcat or the Eagle had even reached the prototype hardware stage.

More than a few Western eyes have been opened, too, by the superb little delta-winged MiG-21, originally viewed almost with disdain as a 'cheap and cheerful' short-range clear-weather day interceptor but which has blossomed into a fully-viable and highly-efficient all-weather multi-purpose warplane. With types such as these, the Sukhoi Su-15 and Tupolev Tu-28P in service, together with the swing-wing Mikoyan MiG-23, the picture of Soviet fighter strength in the early 1970s was a formidable one indeed.

America's realisation that 'jack-of-all-trades' designs like the F-111 are far from being the most effective way to meet the need for an air superiority fighter is as welcome as it is belated. Just how welcome was highlighted in 1970 by McDonnell Douglas, airframe design company for the F-15. It compared the 12-to-1 margin of U.S. air superiority over Soviet fighters which existed in the Korean war to a ratio of about 2·5 to 1 in the air war over Vietnam, attributing this to the U.S.S.R.'s continued devotion to manoeuvrability and acceleration while American multi-purpose fighters have improved chiefly in the realms of range, firepower, weapon load and electronics. As a result the main emphasis in designing the F-15 has been to ensure that it is as first-class a 'dog-fight' aeroplane as possible. The same philosophy can be seen in the little General Dynamics YF-16 and Northrop YF-17 proto-types competing in 1974 for the U.S.A.F's LWF (lightweight fighter) requirement.

Outside of the U.S.A. and U.S.S.R., there are no new 'pure' interceptors on the horizon at all. The R.A.F. continues to use the latest versions of the Lightning in this role, Sweden has the now-ageing J 35F Draken and the Italian Air Force the locally-built F-104S Starfighter; but, excellent though these aircraft are, they all represent virtually the limit of development of designs which originated in the 1950s.

In the area of strike and multi-purpose tactical aircraft, how-ever, the Western picture is much brighter, for warplanes of this type have received far greater attention by nations outside the Soviet bloc.

Aircraft in the strike/attack/close support categories, when they carry a gun armament, are most likely to do so in the form of a packaged pod, complete with ammunition, which may be only one of a score of possible externally-carried 'stores'. Today's attack aircraft can carry a weapon load as great in lethality, and often in sheer physical weight, as any World War 2 heavy bomber, but so much of the space inside a modern combat aircraft is nowadays needed for engines, fuel and complicated avionics that little if any room is left for a weapons bay, and long-suffering airframes must support their weapons on external mountings.

Of the Western fighters already mentioned the Lightning, Mirage and Starfighter have all proved themselves capable of being adapted with considerable success to the strike/attack role, and in the McDonnell Douglas F-4 Phantom and Republic F-105 Thunderchief America undoubtedly has two of the most potent members of the 'Christmas tree brigade' in the world today, even though the Phantom, almost unbelievably, is now twenty years old. Moreover, each of these aircraft, once divested of its offensive loads, ranks as a formidable fighter in its own right. Alongside them must be placed Saab-Scania's AJ 37 Viggen, which entered Swedish Air Force service in 1971 and bids fair to achieve as long an active life as its predecessor, the Draken. At a somewhat lower level of sophistication, though still in a supersonic performance bracket, may be counted the well-proven Northrop F-5; more recent entrants into service are the F-5E, the new Anglo-French Jaguar and Dassault's Mach 2 Mirage F1. Among subsonic Western attack aircraft the Vought A-7 Corsair II has emerged during recent years as an outstanding type.

In the Soviet Union – the birthplace of the *shturmovik* – the principal specialised attack aircraft in current service is the Sukhoi Su-7B; this has been joined in recent years by its swing-wing derivatives, the Su-17 and Su-20, and it seems likely that the latest Soviet ground attack aircraft, code-named 'Fencer', is also a Sukhoi design. Similar duties are also performed by variants of the MiG-19 Farmer and MiG-21 Fishbed fighters, and by light tactical bombers such as the Yak-28 Brewer.

Without doubt the most significant arrival in the strike aircraft arena in recent years has been the Hawker Siddeley Harrier. Unique among operational combat aircraft, the Harrier, which went into service with the Royal Air Force in 1969, has a V/STOL capability which not only makes it independent of fixed bases and prepared runways but enables it to operate from any area, on land or afloat, no bigger than the average domestic back yard. Thus it combines a transonic performance and the weapon-carrying capacity of a fixed-wing attack aircraft with the operational flexibility of a helicopter, and it came as no surprise when it was ordered also by the U.S. Marine Corps, who regard it as ideal for the type of operations in which they must be ready to engage. The Harrier has, as yet, no U.S. counterpart, nor yet a known Soviet one. In 1967 the U.S.S.R. exhibited publicly two Yakovlev Yak-36 prototypes (N.A.T.O. code name Freehand), but these were regarded as primitive by comparison with the Harrier. At the 1967 display the U.S.S.R. also showed a number of prototypes, including variants of the MiG-21 and Sukhoi Su-15, which indicated that STOL capabilities for fighter aircraft were then under consideration. In the ensuing seven years it is quite conceivable that a Soviet counterpart to the Harrier may have been evolved and may appear when next the U.S.S.R. decides to display its latest warplanes publicly.

Among nations whose aircraft industries are smaller or less developed than those of the major powers, fortunes in the 1960s tended to fluctuate. Egypt's Messerschmitt-designed HA-300 fighter, which appeared in the original edition of this volume, was axed in the spring of 1969 just when it was at last on the verge of flying with its definitive engine, and in 1974 Hindustan Aeronautics of India still had not found the engine which it required to enable its Marut fighter to achieve its intended Mach 2 performance. In Japan, Mitsubishi has now flown that country's first nationally-designed supersonic aircraft, the XT-2, while the aircraft industries of both mainland China and offshore Taiwan, though producing no indigenously-designed aircraft, are both increasing their output of foreign types. Expansion is also the order of the day in Argentina and Brazil, the former country having evolved in recent years the Pucará twin-turboprop light attack aircraft among other designs.

As the world's aircraft carrier fleets (apart from that of the United States) continue to dwindle – Canada and the Netherlands have forsaken the carrier altogether, and other fleets have been slimmed down – so correspondingly does the apparent future of the naval fighter *per se*. The only new requirements to emerge in very recent times have been the Grumman F-14 already mentioned and an updated version of the Dassault Etendard for the French Navy. Meanwhile, useful employment continues to be found for such types as the original Dassault Etendard IV and the

Vought F-8 Crusader, though neither of these can any longer be regarded as modern in conception.

While the larger, faster and more expensive categories of warplane owe their existence chiefly to the threat of war on a global scale, there is another which has come very much into the foreground as a result of the all-too-common border disputes, minor conflicts and wars of attrition like that in Vietnam. The aircraft in this 'coin' category (an abbreviation of *co*unter-*in*surgency) are functionally the latter-day equivalent of what was once termed the 'police' or 'colonial' aeroplane. In the days when the duties of such an aircraft consisted chiefly of 'keeping the natives' heads down', elegance of design was generally regarded as an expensive luxury, and as often as not they were ungainly, slow-flying machines whose capabilities were somewhat limited.

Requirements change, however, and it was the Korean war of 1950–53 which laid the foundations of todays' conception of the 'coin' aircraft. Korea was the first full-scale military confrontation in which the opposing elements were equipped with substantial numbers of jet combat aircraft, and preoccupation with, particularly, the rival merits of the MiG-15 and Sabre tended to overshadow the part played in undiminishing numbers by piston-engined types, notably the Douglas Skyraider and Invader, despite the arrival in the fighting areas of more and more jet aircraft. In Algeria, the French also found that the piston-engined type could still have the advantage over the jet in certain applications, and this held true to some extent throughout the unhappy prolongation of hostilities in Vietnam and in other recent trouble-spots. Among the early 'coin' types was the North American T-28, originally designed purely as a training aircraft but converted later to carry a modest load of attack weapons. One of the first items of aerial hardware to be supplied under the programme of U.S. military assistance to the South Vietnamese government, the T-28 remained a useful light attack aircraft until its abilities were generally overtaken by more effective jet types in the general escalation of the war in south-east Asia.

The African continent – at first in Katanga and more recently in the internal struggle between Nigerian federal forces and those of the breakaway province of Biafra – saw the blooding of probably the smallest 'coin' aircraft yet to be produced. This is the Malmö MFI-9, a military version of the diminutive Bölkow Junior lightplane with which hundreds of club and private-owner fliers are familiar as a 'weekend runabout' aeroplane. Yet a score or so of these tiny, 24 ft. 4 in. (7·43 m.) span aircraft, equipped with underwing rocket projectiles and flown by Count Carl Gustav von Rosen's team of mercenaries, provided for many months a nuisance to their opponents that was out of all proportion to their size. Another small-size 'coin' type to appear recently – though not so small as the MFI-9 – was the little Kraguj from Yugoslavia.

The ability to perform the dual roles of attack aircraft and trainer is now, however, almost wholly the prerogative of jet aircraft. Indeed, the jet trainer that does not have a secondary attack capability is nowadays the exception rather than the rule, and the reason is not hard to find. The natural requirements for a training aircraft are that it should be simple to fly, should handle well at medium and low speeds with as few vices as possible, and should be both manoeuvrable and sturdily built. It therefore comes into being already possessed of most of the attributes required for the light attack role. Its robust construction makes it a ready-made platform for external weapon loads, and its manoeuvrability and low-altitude performance give it the ability to make low-level attacks on targets that may be too small or too inaccessible for larger and faster aircraft to attack successfully. In addition, for gunnery training purposes, it is likely to have a built-in gun armament from the outset.

Among the outstanding jet trainer/attack types of recent years are the American Cessna T-37/A-37 and Britain's Jet Provost/Strikemaster family of aircraft. Both types began life purely as trainers, the Jet Provost being the first in the world on which an 'all-through' jet training policy was based, and for many years they served admirably in this role alone. Both have since undergone considerable development, and today can be ranked among the world leaders in this class of aircraft; and the Jet Provost in its latest form remains the primary jet training type of the Royal Air Force. Other noteworthy members of the jet trainer/attack class range from the ubiquitous Aermacchi M.B. 326 – built or assembled in Australia, South Africa and Brazil as well as in Italy – to the Canadair CL-41 and the more recent Saab 105 from Sweden and Galeb/Jastreb from Yugoslavia.

But even if there were not this second side to the trainer's capabilities, it would still represent a class of aeroplane worthy of attention in its own right. Although it may not have the aura of glamour that more usually surrounds the fighter or the bomber, the care and thought which go into its design and construction must be every bit as great as that which goes into a major warplane. This is a natural corollary to the increasing sophistication of the fighter and bomber, which are nowadays so costly as well as so complex that corresponding care must be taken in training the men to whom they will be entrusted.

As the roles of front-line warplanes have become more diverse and more precisely defined, so has the programme of preparation for those who fly in them, and it is quite usual for a present-day combat pilot to go through successive stages of training on perhaps four different aeroplane types before joining an operational squadron. These may consist of basic, intermediate and advanced flying training, followed by a course at an operational conversion unit on a special training version of the particular type of aircraft that he will ultimately fly. Added to this may be several weeks of ground instruction and many hours of 'ground flying' in the appropriate simulator for the ultimate operational type.

When the Jet Provost entered R.A.F. service, pioneering an 'all-through' syllabus of training on jet-driven aircraft, this formula was regarded as the new pattern for the future and was adopted in due course by most of the world's other major air forces. It enabled the student flier to begin right from the start to receive his instruction in a jet aircraft, and reduced total pilot training hours by eliminating the need for him to 'unlearn' piston-engine techniques when transferring to the second phase on jets. This policy has since undergone some revision, however, and nowadays it is considered that a few preliminary hours on a propeller-driven pre-selection trainer is a better way of discovering, at an early stage, those students who are felt to lack the potential to become good pilots. Thus unnecessary expenditure is saved by curtailing sooner the training of an unsuitable candidate. Among the types used or envisaged for pre-selection flying are the Cessna T-41, Scottish Aviation Bulldog, SIAI-Marchetti SF.260 and Saab-MFI 15.

In Eastern Europe, meanwhile, the Aero L-29 Delfin continues to hold the stage as the principal jet trainer of the U.S.S.R. and its associate Warsaw Pact countries, with the exception of Poland, which has preferred its own TS-11 Iskra. However, production of the Delfin is expected to be phased out before long, its place already having begun to be taken in the Czechoslovak Air Force by the more modern L-39, which will also be supplied to other Warsaw Pact nations including the U.S.S.R. For the time being Britain, France and Germany continue to rely, respectively, on the Jet Provost, Gnat and Super Magister, while the needs of the Spanish Air Force are met by the HA-200 E and of Sweden by the Saab 105. France and Germany are currently developing a mutually-needed Magister replacement in the form of the Dassault-Breguet/Dornier Alpha Jet, and Britain's Gnat Trainers will eventually be replaced by the new Hawker Siddeley Hawk. Meanwhile the needs of the U.S. Navy and Air Force continue to be met adequately by the T-2 Buckeye and the T-38 Talon – the latter, which has been in service since 1961, still being the world's only supersonic 'pure' training aircraft in service.

THE COLOUR PLATES

As an aid to identification, the eighty colour pages which follow have been arranged in an essentially visual order, within the broad sequence: piston-engined aircraft, straight-winged and swept-winged jet aircraft. The reference number of each aircraft corresponds to the appropriate text matter. An index to all types appears on pages 173–175.

The 'split' plan view, adopted to give both upper and lower surface markings within a single plan outline, depicts the colour scheme appearing above and below either the port or starboard half of the aircraft, according to whichever aspect is shown in the side elevation.

CESSNA T-41 (U.S.A.)

Cessna T-41A Mescalero of the Fuerza Aérea del Peru, *ca* 1967. *Engine:* One 145 hp Continental O-300-C six-cylinder horizontally-opposed type. *Span:* 36 ft 2in. (11·02 m). *Length:* 26 ft 6 in. (8·07 m). *Wing area:* 174·0 sq ft (16·165 sq m). *Maximum take-off weight:* 2,300 lb (1,043 kg). *Maximum speed:* 139 mph (224 km/hr) at sea level. *Service ceiling:* 13,100 ft (3,995 m). *Maximum range:* 640 miles (1,030 km).

DORNIER Do 27 (Germany)

2

Dornier Do 27A-4 of the Luftwaffe, *ca* 1963. *Engine:* One 270 hp Lycoming GO-480-B six-cylinder horizontally-opposed type. *Span:* 39 ft 4½ in. (12·00 m). *Length:* 31 ft 6 in. (9·60 m). *Wing area:* 208·8 sq ft (19·40 sq m). *Normal take-off weight:* 4,070 lb (1,850 kg). *Maximum speed:* 141 mph (227 km/hr) at 3,280 ft (1,000 m). *Service ceiling:* 10,825 ft (3,300 m). *Range with internal fuel:* 685 miles (1,100 km).

KRAGUJ (Yugoslavia)

3

Soko P-2 Kraguj in the insignia of the Jugoslovensko Ratno Vazduhoplovstvo, *ca* summer 1968. *Engine:* One 340 hp Lycoming GSO-480-B1A6 six-cylinder horizontally-opposed type. *Span:* 34 ft 11 in. (10·64 m). *Length:* 26 ft $0\frac{1}{4}$ in. (7·93 m). *Wing area:* 183·0 sq ft (17·00 sq m). *Maximum take-off weight:* 3,580 lb (1,624 kg). *Maximum speed:* 183 mph (295 km/hr) at 4,925 ft (1,500 m). *Maximum range with standard fuel:* 495 miles (800 km).

BULLDOG (U.K.)

4

Scottish Aviation Bulldog Model 103 of the Kenya Air Force, 1972. *Engine:* One 200 hp Lycoming IO-360-A1B6 four-cylinder horizontally-opposed type. *Span:* 33 ft 0 in. (10·06 m). *Length:* 23 ft 3 in. (7·09 m). *Wing area:* 129·4 sq ft. (12·02 sq m). *Maximum take-off weight:* 2,350 lb. (1,066 kg). *Maximum speed:* 150 mph (241 km/hr) at sea level. *Service ceiling:* 17,000 ft (5,180 m). *Maximum range:* 621 miles (1,000 km).

MENTOR (U.S.A.)

5

Beechcraft T-34A Mentor of the Japan Air Self-Defence Force (11th Training Unit), *ca* 1962–63. *Engine:* One 225 hp Continental O-470-13 six-cylinder horizontally-opposed type. *Span:* 32 ft 10 in. (10·00 m). *Length:* 25 ft 11¼ in. (7·91 m). *Wing area:* 177·6 sq ft (16·50 sq m). *Normal take-off weight:* 2,950 lb (1,338 kg). *Maximum speed:* 189 mph (304 km/hr) at sea level. *Service ceiling:* 20,000 ft (6,100 m). *Range with internal fuel:* 735 miles (1,180 km).

T-28 (U.S.A.)

6

North American T-28A of the Republic of Korea Air Force, *ca* 1961–62. *Engine:* One 800 hp Wright R-1300-1A Cyclone seven-cylinder radial. *Span:* 40 ft 1 in. (12·22 m). *Length:* 32 ft 0 in. (9·75 m). *Wing area:* 268·0 sq ft (24·90 sq m). *Normal take-off weight:* 6,365 lb (2,887 kg). *Maximum speed:* 283 mph (455 km/hr) at 5,900 ft (1,800 m). *Service ceiling:* 24,000 ft (7,315 m). *Range on internal fuel:* 1,000 miles (1,610 km).

YAKOVLEV Yak-18 (U.S.S.R.)

7

Yakovlev Yak-18A (Max) of the DOSAAF, 1966. *Engine:* One 260 hp Ivchenko AI-14R nine-cylinder radial. *Span:* 34 ft 9¼ in. (10·60 m). *Length:* 27 ft 4¾ in. (8·35 m). *Wing area:* 191·6 sq ft (17·80 sq m). *Take-off weight:* 2,901 lb (1,316 kg). *Maximum speed:* 162 mph (260 km/hr). *Service ceiling:* 16,600 ft (5,060 m). *Range:* 465 miles (750 km).

YAKOVLEV Yak-11 (U.S.S.R.)

8

Czechoslovak-built C.11 (Yak-11 Moose) of the United Arab Republic Air Force, flown to Israel in January 1964 by Captain Hekmi. *Engine:* One 730 hp Shvetsov ASh-21 seven-cylinder radial. *Span:* 30 ft 10 in. (9·40 m). *Length:* 27 ft 10¾ in. (8·50 m). *Wing area:* 165·8 sq ft (15·40 sq m). *Normal take-off weight:* 5,512 lb (2,500 kg). *Maximum speed:* 286 mph (460 km/hr) at 7,380 ft (2,250 m). *Service ceiling:* 23,300 ft (7,100 m). *Range on internal fuel:* 795 miles (1,280 km).

PIAGGIO P.149 (Italy)

9

Piaggio P. 149U of the Uganda Army Air Force, *ca* 1968. *Engine:* One 270 hp Piaggio-built Lycoming GO-480-B1A6 six-cylinder horizontally-opposed type. *Span:* 36 ft 5¾ in. (11·12 m). *Length:* 28 ft 10¾ in. (8·85 m). *Wing area:* 202·5 sq ft (18·81 sq m). *Take-off weight:* 3,704 lb (1,680 kg). *Maximum speed:* 189 mph (304 km/hr) at sea level. *Service ceiling:* 16,400 ft (5,000 m). *Maximum range:* 675 miles (1,090 km).

SF.260MX (Italy)

10

SIAI-Marchetti SF.260MB of the Force Aérienne Belge, ca 1971. *Engine:* One 260 hp Lycoming O-540-E4A5 six-cylinder horizontally-opposed type. *Span:* 27 ft 0¾ in. (8·25 m). *Length:* 23 ft 3½ in. (7·10 m). *Wing area:* 108·7 sq ft. (10·10 sq m). *Maximum take-off weight:* 2,998 lb (1,360 kg). *Maximum speed:* 211 mph (340 km/hr) at sea level. *Service ceiling:* 16,400 ft (5,000 m). *Maximum range:* 895 miles (1,440 km).

HUANQUERO (Argentina)

11

FMA I.A.35-lb Huanquero of the Fuerza Aérea Argentina (I Attack and Exploration Group), ca 1968–69. *Engines:* Two 650 hp I.A.R.-19 El Indio nine-cylinder radials. *Span:* 64 ft $3\frac{3}{4}$ in. (19·60 m). *Length:* 45 ft $10\frac{1}{2}$ in. (13·98 m). *Wing area:* 452·1 sq ft (42·00 sq m). *Take-off weight:* 12,787 lb (5,800 kg). *Maximum speed:* 236 mph (380 km/hr) at 6,900 ft (2,100 m). *Service ceiling:* 22,975 ft (7,000 m). *Range:* 775 miles (1,250 km).

PUCARÁ (Argentina)

12

FMA I.A.58 Pucará second prototype, 1972. *Engines:* Two 1,022 ehp Turboméca Astazou XVI G turboprops. *Span:* 47 ft 6¾ in. (14·50 m). *Length:* 46 ft 3 in. (14·10 m). *Wing area:* 326·1 sq ft (30·30 sq m). *Maximum take-off weight:* 14,300 lb (6,486 kg). *Maximum speed:* 323 mph (520 km/hr) at 9,840 ft (3,000 m). *Service ceiling:* 27,165 ft (8,280 m). *Range with maximum fuel:* 1,890 miles (3,042 km).

AÉROSPATIALE N 262 (France)

13

Aérospatiale N 262 Series A of the Aéronautique Navale, 1969. *Engines:* Two 1,065 ehp Turboméca Bastan VIC turboprops. *Span:* 71 ft 10 in. (21·90 m). *Length:* 63 ft 3 in. (19·28 m). *Wing area:* 592·0 sq ft (55·00 sq m). *Maximum take-off weight:* 23,369 lb (10,600 kg). *Maximum speed:* 239 mph (385 km/hr). *Service ceiling:* 19,200 ft (5,850 m). *Range with 4,343 lb (1,970 kg) payload:* 755 miles (1,220 km).

JETSTREAM (U.K.)

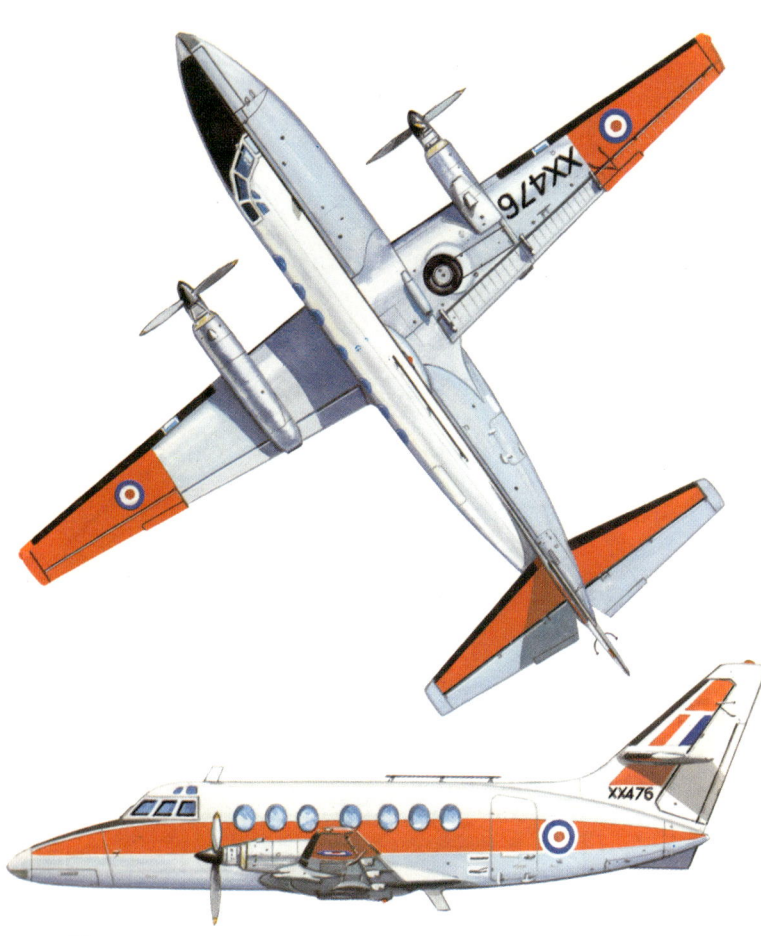

14

Scottish Aviation Jetstream T. Mk 1 (Model 201), second production aircraft for the RAF, 1973. *Engines:* Two 996 ehp Turboméca Astazou XVI D turboprops. *Span:* 52 ft 0 in. (15·85 m). *Length:* 47 ft 1½ in. (14·36 m). *Wing area:* 270·0 sq ft (25·08 sq m). *Maximum take-off weight:* 12,566 lb (5,700 kg). *Maximum speed:* 282 mph (454 km/hr) at 10,000 ft (3,050 m). *Service ceiling:* 26,000 ft (7,925 m). *Maximum range, with reserves:* 1,380 miles (2,220 km).

STARFIGHTER (U.S.A.)

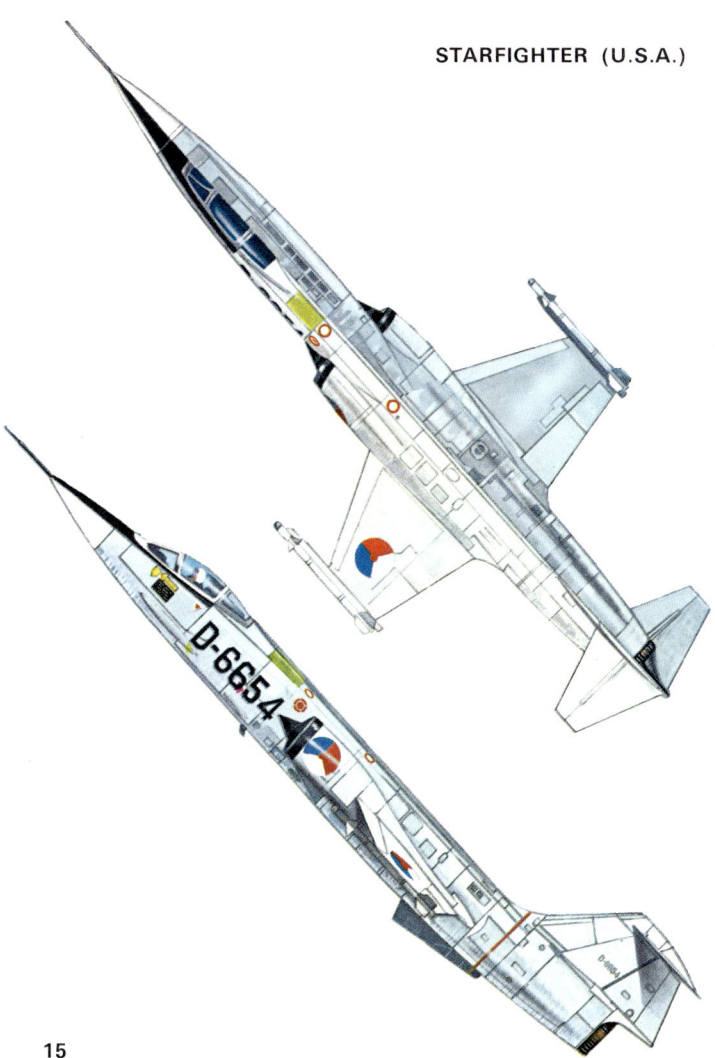

15

Fiat-built Lockheed F-104G Starfighter of the Koninklijke Luchtmacht (No 323 Squadron), 1964. *Engine:* One 10,000/15,800 lb (4,536/7,167 kg) st General Electric J79-GE-11A afterburning turbojet. *Span:* 21 ft 11 in. (6·68 m). *Length:* 54 ft 9 in. (16·69 m). *Wing area:* 196·1 sq ft (18·22 sq m). *Normal take-off weight:* 19,841 lb (9,000 kg). *Maximum speed:* 1,320 mph (2,125 km/hr) above 36,000 ft (11,000 m). *Service ceiling:* 55,000 ft (16,765 m). *Typical operational radius:* 690 miles (1,110 km).

TALON (U.S.A.)

16

Northrop T-38A Talon of the US Air Force (Air Training Command), *ca* 1961–62. *Engines:* Two 2,680/3,850 lb (1,216/1,748 kg) st General Electric J85-GE-5 afterburning turbojets. *Span:* 25 ft 3 in. (7·70 m). *Length:* 46 ft 4½ in. (14·13 m). *Wing area:* 170·0 sq ft (15·79 sq m). *Maximum take-off weight:* 12,050 lb (5,465 kg). *Maximum speed:* 820 mph (1,320 km/hr) above 36,000 ft (11,000 m). *Service ceiling:* 53,600 ft (16,335 m). *Maximum range:* 1,100 miles (1,770 km).

NORTHROP F-5 (U.S.A.)

17

Northrop F-5A of the Republic of Korea Air Force (10th Fighter Wing), 1965. *Engines:* Two 2,720/4,080 lb (1,234/1,850 kg) st General Electric J85-GE-13 afterburning turbojets. *Span:* 25 ft 3 in. (7·70 m). *Length:* 47 ft 2 in. (14·38 m). *Wing area:* 170·0 sq ft (15·79 sq m). *Maximum take-off weight:* 20,576 lb (9,333 kg). *Maximum speed at all-up weight of 11,450 lb (5,193 kg):* 925 mph (1,489 km/hr) above 36,000 ft (11,000 m). *Service ceiling:* over 50,000 ft (15,250 m). *Typical combat radius:* 550 miles (885 km).

TIGER II (U.S.A.)

18

Northrop F-5E Tiger II, tenth production aircraft for the USAF, as displayed at the Paris Air Show, May/June 1973. *Engines:* Two 3,500/5,000 lb (1,588/2,268 kg) st General Electric J85-GE-21 afterburning turbojets. *Span over missiles:* 27 ft 11⅞ in. (8·53 m). *Length:* 48 ft 3¾ in. (14·73 m). *Wing area:* 186·0 sq ft. (17·28 sq m). *Maximum take-off weight:* 24,080 lb (10,922 kg). *Maximum speed:* 1,058 mph (1,703 km/hr) at 36,000 ft (11,000 m). *Service ceiling:* 54,000 ft (16,460 m). *Combat radius with maximum fuel and two Sidewinders:* 875 miles (1,408 km).

LOCKHEED T-33A (U.S.A.)

19

Lockheed T-33A of the Royal Thai Air Force (1st Wing), *ca* 1963. *Engine:* One 5,400 lb (2,449 kg) st Allison J33-A-35 turbojet. *Span:* 38 ft 10½ in. (11·85 m). *Length:* 37 ft 9 in. (11·51 m). *Wing area:* 237·0 sq ft (22·02 sq m). *Normal take-off weight:* 11,965 lb (5,428 kg). *Maximum speed:* 600 mph (966 km/hr) at sea level. *Service ceiling:* 47,500 ft (14,480 m). *Range:* 1,345 miles (2,165 km).

MAGISTER (France)

Aérospatiale (Fouga) Magister of the Force Aérienne Belge, *ca* 1964. *Engines:* Two 880 lb (400 kg) st Turboméca Marboré IIA turbojets. *Span over tip-tanks:* 39 ft 10¼ in. (12·15 m). *Length:* 33 ft 0 in. (10·06 m). *Wing area:* 186·2 sq ft (17·30 sq m). *Normal take-off weight:* 6,834 lb (3,100 kg). *Maximum speed:* 444 mph (715 km/hr) at 29,525 ft (9,000 m). *Service ceiling:* 36,000 ft (11,000 m). *Range with underwing fuel tanks:* 745 miles (1,200 km).

SAETA (Spain)

Hispano E-14 Saeta (HA-200 D) of the Ejercito del Aire (Escuela de Reacción), 1965. *Engines:* Two 880 lb (400 kg) st Turboméca Marboré IIA turbojets. *Span:* 35 ft 10¼ in. (10·93 m). *Length:* 29 ft 5¼ in. (8·97 m). *Wing area:* 187·3 sq ft (17·40 sq m). *Maximum take-off weight:* 7,385 lb (3,350 kg). *Maximum speed:* 404 mph (650 km/hr) at sea level. *Service ceiling:* 39,375 ft (12,000 m). *Range with maximum fuel:* 930 miles (1,500 km).

BUCKEYE (U.S.A.)

Rockwell International (North American) T-2A Buckeye of the US Navy (Air Basic Training Command), *ca* 1963. *Engine:* One 3,400 lb (1,540 kg) st Westinghouse J34-WE-36 turbojet. *Span over tip-tanks:* 37 ft $10\frac{1}{4}$ in. (11·54 m). *Length:* 38 ft $3\frac{1}{2}$ in. (11·67 m). *Wing area:* 255·0 sq ft (23·69 sq m). *Maximum take-off weight:* 11,373 lb (5,159 kg). *Maximum speed:* 492 mph (792 km/hr) at 25,000 ft (7,620 m). *Service ceiling:* 42,500 ft (12,955 m). *Range with tip-tanks:* 965 miles (1,555 km).

KIRAN (India)

HAL HJT-16 Kiran Mk I of the Indian Air Force, *ca* 1972. *Engine:* One 2,500 lb (1,135 kg) st Rolls-Royce Bristol Viper 11 turbojet. *Span:* 35 ft 1¼ in. (10·70 m). *Length:* 34 ft 9 in. (10·60 m). *Wing area:* 204·5 sq ft (19·00 sq m). *Normal take-off weight:* 7,936 lb (3,600 kg). *Maximum speed:* 432 mph (695 km/hr) at sea level. *Service ceiling:* 30,000 ft (9,850 m). *Range on internal fuel:* 466 miles (750 km).

ISKRA (Poland)

WSK-Mielec TS-11 Iskra of the Polskie Lotnictwo Wojskowe, *ca* 1967–68. *Engine:* One 2,205 lb (1,000 kg) st Instytut Lotnictwa SO-3 turbojet. *Span:* 33 ft 0¼ in. (10·07 m). *Length:* 36 ft 10¾ in. (11·25 m). *Wing area:* 188·4 sq ft (17·50 sq m). *Normal take-off weight:* 8,068 lb (3,660 kg). *Maximum speed:* 447 mph (720 km/hr) at 16,400 ft (5,000 m). *Service ceiling:* 41,000 ft (12,500 m). *Maximum range:* 907 miles (1,460 km).

TUTOR (Canada)

25

Canadair CL-41A (CT-114 Tutor) of the Royal Canadian Air Force (Training Command), 1964. *Engine:* One 2,633 lb (1,194 kg) st General Electric J85-Can-40 (CJ610-1B) turbojet. *Span:* 36 ft 6 in. (11·13 m). *Length:* 32 ft 0 in. (9·75 m). *Wing area:* 220·0 sq ft (20·44 sq m). *Normal take-off weight:* 7,397 lb (3,355 kg). *Maximum speed:* 486 mph (782 km/hr) at 27,500 ft (8,380 m). *Service ceiling:* 43,000 ft (13,105 m). *Normal range:* 945 miles (1,520 km).

AERMACCHI M.B.326 (Italy)

26

Aermacchi M.B.326 of the Aeronautica Militare Italiano (Scuola Volo Periodo Basico), *ca* 1962–63. *Engine:* One 2,500 lb (1,135 kg) st Rolls-Royce Bristol Viper 11 Mk 22 turbojet. *Span:* 34 ft 8 in. (10·56 m). *Length:* 34 ft $11\frac{1}{4}$ in. (10·65 m). *Wing area:* 204·5 sq ft (19·00 sq m). *Maximum take-off weight:* 8,300 lb (3,765 kg). *Maximum speed:* 501 mph (806 km/hr) at 15,000 ft (4,575 m). *Service ceiling:* 41,000 ft (12,500 m). *Range with underwing fuel tanks:* 1,245 miles (2,000 km).

DELFIN (Czechoslovakia)

27

Aero L-29 Delfin of the Iraqi Air Force, *ca* 1968. *Engine:* One 1,962 lb (890 kg) st Motorlet M 701c 500 turbojet. *Span:* 33 ft 9 in. (10·29 m). *Length:* 35 ft 5½ in. (10·81 m). *Wing area:* 213·1 sq ft (19·80 sq m). *Normal take-off weight:* 7,231 lb (3,280 kg). *Maximum speed:* 407 mph (655 km/hr) at 16,400 ft (5,000 m). *Service ceiling:* 36,000 ft (11,000 m). *Range with underwing fuel tanks:* 555 miles (894 km).

AERO L-39 (Czechoslovakia)

Aero L-39 in the insignia of the Ceskoslovénské Letectvo, 1973. *Engine:* One 3,792 lb (1,720 kg) st Walter Titan (Motorlet-built Ivchenko AI-25-TL) turbofan. *Span:* 31 ft 0½ in. (9·46 m). *Length:* 40 ft 5 in. (12·32 m). *Wing area:* 202·4 sq ft (18·80 sq m). *Normal take-off weight:* 9,083 lb (4,120 kg). *Maximum speed:* 466 mph (750 km/hr) at 16,400 ft (5,000 m). *Service ceiling:* 37,075 ft (11,300 m). *Normal range:* 677 miles (1,090 km).

CESSNA A-37 (U.S.A)

29

Cessna A-37A of the US Air Force (604th Air Commando Squadron, Bien Hoa, Vietnam), *ca* 1967–68. *Engines:* Two 2,450 lb (1,111 kg) st General Electric J85-GE-17A. *Remaining data apply to A-37B. Span:* 35 ft 10½ in. (10·93 m). *Length:* 29 ft 3½ in. (8·93 m). *Wing area:* 183·9 sq ft (17·09 sq m). *Maximum take-off weight:* 12,000 lb (5,443 kg). *Maximum speed:* 478 mph (769 km/hr) at sea level. *Service ceiling:* 41,765 ft (12,730 m). *Range with 3,700 lb (1,678 kg) of external stores:* 250 miles (402 km).

JASTREB (Yugoslavia)

Soko J-1 Jastreb second prototype, in the insignia of the Jugoslovensko Ratno Vazduhoplovstvo, summer 1968. *Engine:* One 3,000 lb (1,360 kg) st Rolls-Royce Bristol Viper 531 turbojet. *Span over tip-tanks:* 38 ft 4 in. (11·68 m). *Length:* 35 ft 1½ in. (10·71 m). *Wing area:* 204·5 sq ft (19·00 sq m). *Maximum take-off weight (clean):* 8,748 lb (3,968 kg). *Maximum speed:* 510 mph (820 km/hr) at 19,685 ft (6,000 m). *Service ceiling:* 39,375 ft (12,000 m). *Maximum range with standard fuel:* 945 miles (1,520 km).

JET PROVOST (U.K.)

31

BAC Jet Provost T. Mk 51 of the Royal Ceylon Air Force, *ca* 1964. *Engine:* One 1,750 lb (795 kg) st Rolls-Royce Bristol Viper Mk 102 turbojet. *Span:* 36 ft 11 in. (11·25 m). *Length:* 32 ft 5 in. (9·88 m). *Wing area:* 213·7 sq ft (19·85 sq m). *Normal take-off weight:* 7,910 lb (3,588 kg). *Maximum speed:* 342 mph (550 km/hr) at 20,000 ft (6,100 m). *Service ceiling:* 21,700 ft (6,610 m). *Typical operational radius:* 330 miles (530 km).

STRIKEMASTER (U.K.)

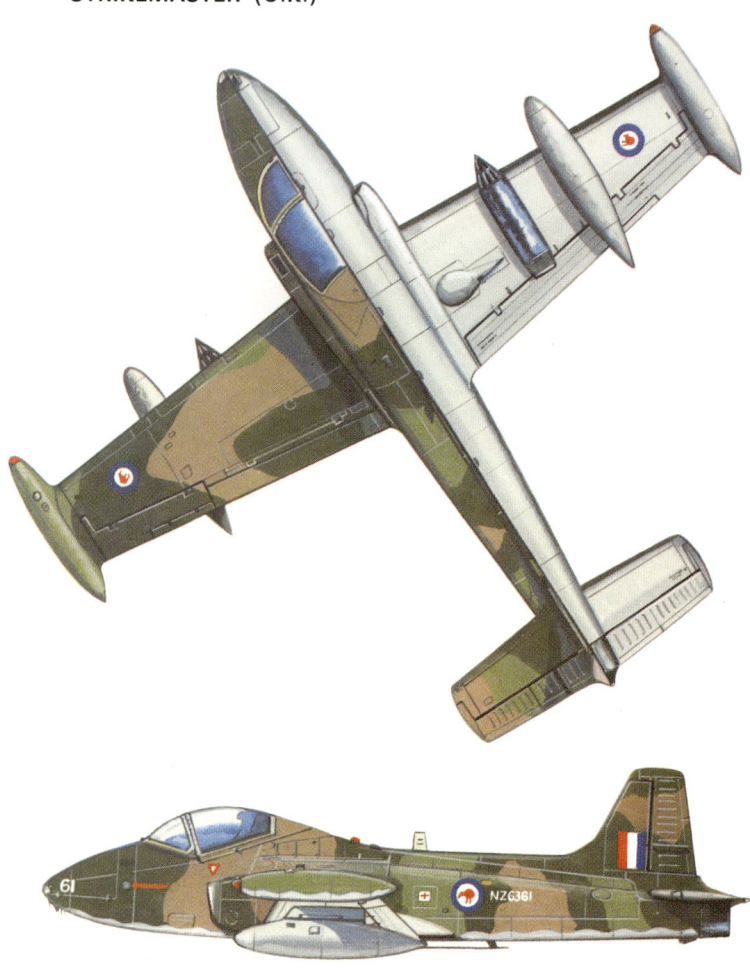

32

BAC 167 Strikemaster Mk 88 of No. 14 Squadron, Royal New Zealand Air Force, *ca* 1971. *Engine:* One 3,410 lb (1,547 kg) st Rolls-Royce Bristol Viper Srs 20 Mk 535 turbojet. *Span:* 36 ft 10 in. (11·23 m). *Length:* 33 ft 8½ in. (10·27 m). *Wing area:* 213·7 sq ft (19·85 sq m). *Maximum take-off weight:* 11,500 lb (5,216 kg). *Maximum speed:* 481 mph (774 km/hr) at 18,000 ft (5,485 m). *Service ceiling:* 40,000 ft (12,200 m). *Range:* 1,382 miles (2,224 km).

SAAB 105 (Sweden)

33

Saab 105Ö, first aircraft for the Österreichische Luftstreitkräfte, spring 1970. *Engines:* Two 2,850 lb (1,293 kg) st General Electric J85-GE-17B turbojets. *Span:* 31 ft 2 in. (9·50 m). *Length:* 35 ft 5¼ in. (10·80 m). *Wing area:* 175·0 sq ft (16·30 sq m). *Maximum take-off weight:* 14,330 lb (6,500 kg). *Maximum speed:* 603 mph (970 km/hr) at sea level. *Service ceiling:* approx 45,000 ft (13,700 m). *Typical attack radius with 3,000 lb (1,360 kg) load:* 514 miles (827 km).

VAMPIRE TRAINER (U.K.)

34

de Havilland D.H.115 Vampire Trainer of the Ilmavoimat (Lennosto 2), *ca* 1958. *Engine:* One 3,500 lb (1,588 kg) st de Havilland Goblin 35 turbojet. *Span:* 38 ft 0 in. (11·58 m). *Length:* 34 ft 6½ in. (10·53 m). *Wing area:* 262·0 sq ft (24·34 sq m). *Normal take-off weight:* 11,150 lb (5,058 kg). *Maximum speed:* 549 mph (884 km/hr) at 20,000 ft (6,100 m). *Service ceiling:* 40,000 ft (12,200 m). *Maximum range:* 853 miles (1,373 km).

SABRE (U.S.A.)

35

North American F-86K-10-NA Sabre of the Konelige Norske Flyvåpen (No 337 Squadron), *ca* 1960. *Engine:* One 5,425/7,500 lb (2,460/3,402 kg) st General Electric J47-GE-17B afterburning turbojet. *Span:* 37 ft 1½ in. (11·32 m). *Length:* 40 ft 11 in. (12·47 m). *Wing area:* 287·9 sq ft (26·75 sq m). *Maximum take-off weight:* 19,952 lb (9,050 kg). *Maximum speed:* 612 mph (985 km/hr) above 36,000 ft (11,000 m). *Service ceiling:* 49,600 ft (15,120 m). *Maximum range with external tanks:* 745 miles (1,200 km).

SUPER SABRE (U.S.A.)

36

North American F-100D Super Sabre of the 308th Tactical Fighter Squadron, 31st Tactical Fighter Wing, USAF, Vietnam 1969–70. *Engine:* One 11,700/16,950 lb (5,307/7,688 kg) st Pratt & Whitney J57-P-21A afterburning turbojet. *Span:* 38 ft 9¾ in. (11·82 m). *Length (excluding probe):* 49 ft 4 in. (15·04 m). *Wing area:* 385·2 sq ft (35·79 sq m). *Normal take-off weight:* 34,050 lb (15,445 kg). *Maximum speed:* 910 mph (1,464 km/hr) at 35,000 ft (10,670 m). *Service ceiling:* 36,000 ft (11,000 m). *Radius on internal fuel:* 534 miles (860 km).

HUNTER (U.K.)

37

Hawker Hunter Mk 57 of the Kuwait Air Force, *ca* 1965. *Engine:* One 10,000 lb (4,536 kg) st Rolls-Royce Avon 203 turbojet. *Span:* 33 ft 8 in. (10·26 m). *Length:* 45 ft 10½ in. (13·98 m). *Wing area:* 349·0 sq ft (32·42 sq m). *Maximum take-off weight:* 24,000 lb (10,886 kg). *Maximum speed:* 710 mph (1,143 km/hr) at sea level. *Service ceiling:* 51,500 ft (15,695 m). *Maximum range with external tanks:* 1,840 miles (2,960 km).

38

Hawker Hunter T. Mk 8, personal transport of the Flag Officer Naval Flying Training, Royal Navy, *ca* 1965. *Engine:* One 7,550 lb (3,425 kg) st Rolls-Royce Avon 122 turbojet. *Span and wing area:* as above. *Length:* 48 ft 10½ in. (14·90 m). *Normal take-off weight:* 17,200 lb (7,802 kg). *Maximum speed:* 710 mph (1,143 km/hr) at 20,000 ft (6,100 m). *Service ceiling:* 47,000 ft (14,325 m). *Range with underwing fuel tanks:* approx 1,650 miles (2,655 km).

LANSEN (Sweden)

39

Saab A 32A Lansen of the Flygvapnet (Flygflottilje 6, Karlsborg), *ca* 1959–60. *Engine:* One 7,937/9,920 lb (3,600/4,500 kg) st Rolls-Royce/Svenska Flygmotor RM5 afterburning turbojet. *Span:* 42 ft 7¾ in. (13·00 m). *Length:* 48 ft 0¾ in. (14·65 m). *Wing area:* 402·6 sq ft (37·40 sq m). *Maximum take-off weight:* 28,660 lb (13,000 kg). *Maximum speed:* 700 mph (1,125 km/hr) at sea level. *Service ceiling:* 49,200 ft (15,000 m). *Typical operational radius:* 745 miles (1,200 km).

FUJI T-1 (Japan)

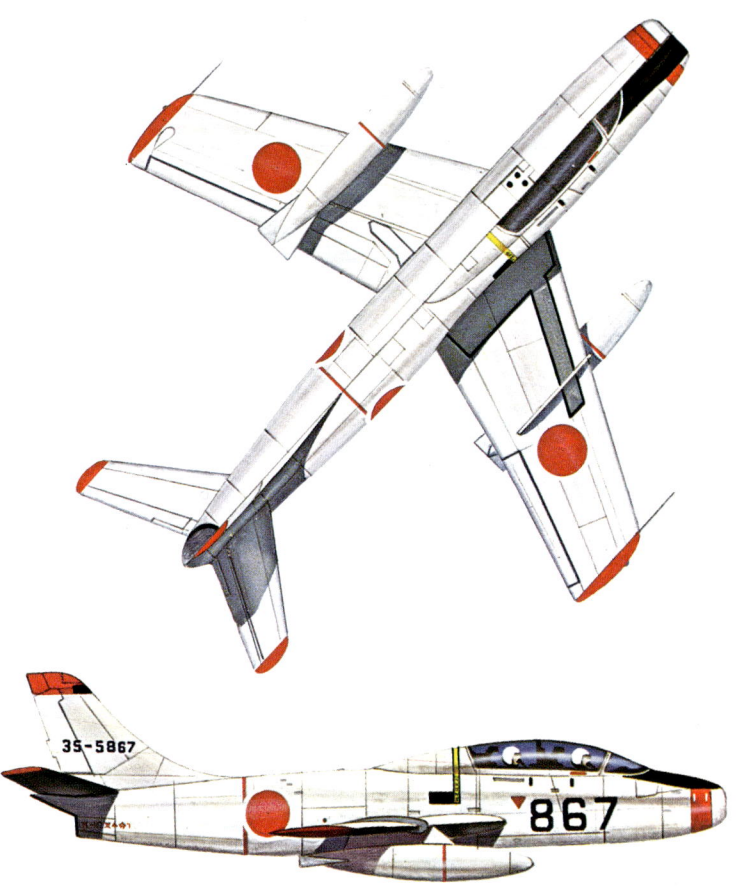

40

Fuji T-1B of the Japan Air Self-Defence Force, *ca* 1963. *Engine:* One 2,645 lb (1,200 kg) st Ishikawajima-Harima J3-IHI-3 turbojet. *Span:* 34 ft 5½ in. (10·50 m). *Length:* 39 ft 9¼ in. (12·12 m). *Wing area:* 239·2 sq ft (22·22 sq m). *Maximum take-off weight:* 11,023 lb (5,000 kg). *Maximum speed:* 518 mph (834 km/hr) at 19,685 ft (6,000 m). *Service ceiling:* 39,375 ft (12,000 m). *Range with underwing fuel tanks:* 1,210 miles (1,950 km).

MiG-17 (U.S.S.R.)

41

Mikoyan/Gurevich MiG-17PF (Fresco-D) of the Angkatan Udara Republik Indonesia, *ca* 1960. *Engine:* One 5,732/7,452 lb (2,600/3,380 kg) st Klimov VK-1F afterburning turbojet. *Span:* 31 ft 6¾ in. (9·62 m). *Length:* 37 ft 8¾ in. (11·50 m). *Wing area:* 243·3 sq ft (22·60 sq m). *Normal take-off weight:* 12,390 lb (5,620 kg). *Maximum speed:* 693 mph (1,115 km/hr) at 9,845 ft (3,000 m). *Service ceiling:* 54,460 ft (16,600 m). *Range with underwing tanks:* approx 1,285 miles (2,070 km).

SUPER MYSTÈRE (France)

42

Dassault Super Mystère B-2 of the Armée de l'Air (5e Escadre of the Défense Aérienne), *ca* 1963. *Engine:* One 7,495/9,700 lb (3,400/4,400 kg) st SNECMA Atar 101G afterburning turbojet. *Span:* 34 ft 5¾ in. (10·51 m). *Length:* 46 ft 1¼ in. (14·05 m). *Wing area:* 376·7 sq ft (35·00 sq m). *Maximum take-off weight:* 22,046 lb (10,000 kg). *Maximum speed:* 743 mph (1,195 km/hr) above 36,000 ft (11,000 m). *Service ceiling:* 55,775 ft (17,000 m). *Range with underwing fuel tanks:* 730 miles (1,175 km).

ÉTENDARD IV (France)

43

Dassault Étendard IV-M of the Aéronautique Navale (Flottille 15F, aircraft carrier *Foch*), *ca* 1967. *Engine:* One 9,700 lb (4,400 kg) st SNECMA Atar 8B turbojet. *Span:* 31 ft 6 in. (9·60 m). *Length:* 47 ft 3 in. (14·40 m). *Wing area:* 312·15 sq ft (29·00 sq m). *Maximum take-off weight:* 22,652 lb (10,275 kg). *Maximum speed:* 674 mph (1,085 km/hr) above 36,000 ft (11,000 m). *Service ceiling:* 49,210 ft (15,000 m). *Tactical radius at high altitude:* 435 miles (700 km).

MiG-19 (U.S.S.R.)

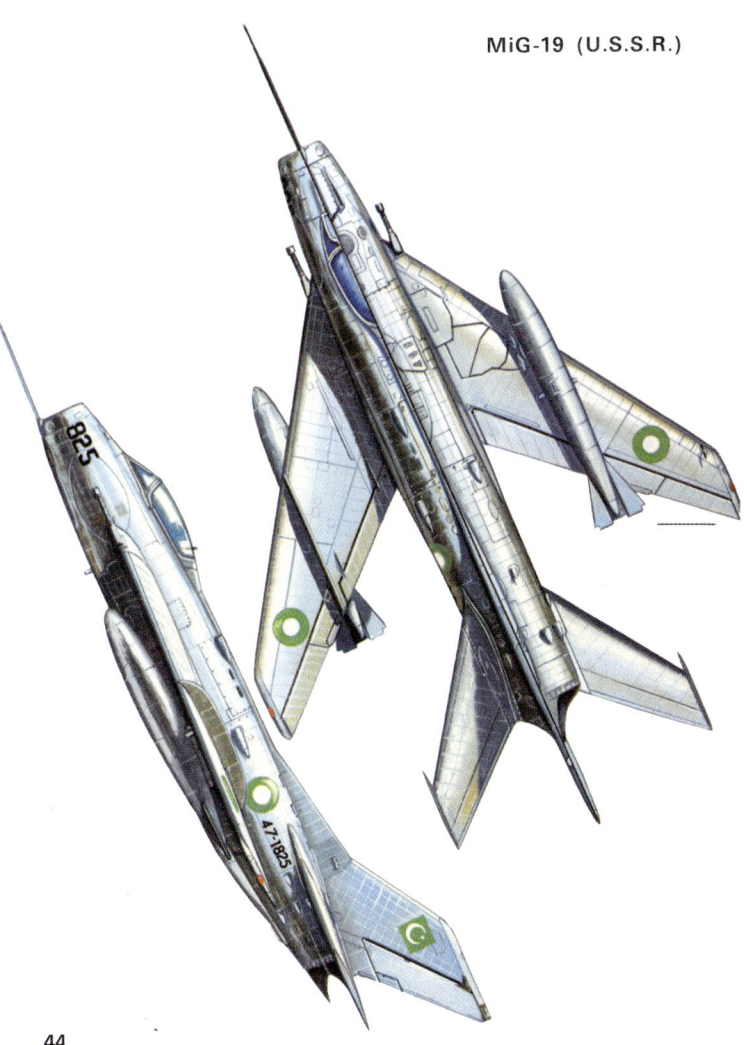

44

Chinese-built Shenyang F-6 (Mikoyan MiG-19SF Farmer-C) of the Pakistan Air Force, 1968. *Engines:* Two 5,732/7,165 lb (2,600/3,250 kg) st RD-9B afterburning turbojets. *Span:* 29 ft 6¾ in. (9·00 m). *Length (excluding nose probe):* 41 ft 1¾ in. (12·54 m). *Wing area:* 269·1 sq ft (25·00 sq m). *Maximum take-off weight:* 19,180 lb (8,700 kg). *Maximum speed:* 902 mph (1,452 km/hr) at 32,800 ft (10,000 m). *Service ceiling:* 58,725 ft (17,900 m). *Combat radius with two underwing tanks:* 425 miles (685 km).

SUKHOI Su-7 (U.S.S.R.)

45

Sukhoi Su-7BM (Fitter-A) of the Polskie Lotnictwo Wojskowe, *ca* 1971. *Engine:* One approx 15,432/22,046 lb (7,000/10,000 kg) st Lyulka AL-7F afterburning turbojet; provision for two JATO bottles. *Span:* 31 ft 11¾ in. (9·75 m). *Length (including nose probe):* 60 ft 8¼ in. (18·50 m). *Height:* 15 ft 9 in. (4·80 m). *Maximum take-off weight:* 29,762 lb (13,500 kg). *Maximum speed:* 1,055 mph (1,700 km/hr) above 36,000 ft (11,000 m). *Service ceiling:* 49,700 ft (15,150 m). *Maximum combat radius:* 300 miles (480 km). *All data estimated.*

GNAT (U.K.)

46

Hawker Siddeley Gnat Mk 1 fighter of the Ilmavoimat (HavLv 21), *ca* 1959–60. *Engine:* One 4,520 lb (2,050 kg) st Rolls-Royce Bristol Orpheus 701 turbojet. *Span:* 22 ft 2 in. (6·75 m). *Length:* 29 ft 9 in. (9·06 m). *Wing area:* 136·6 sq ft (12·69 sq m). *Normal take-off weight:* 6,650 lb (3,016 kg). *Maximum speed:* 695 mph (1,118 km/hr) at 20,000 ft (6,100 m). *Service ceiling:* 50,000 ft (15,000 m). *Radius with underwing fuel tanks:* 500 miles (805 km).

GNAT TRAINER (U.K.)

47

Hawker Siddeley Gnat T. Mk 1 of the RAF ('Red Arrows' aerobatic team), *ca* 1967–68. *Engine:* One 4,400 lb (1,996 kg) st Rolls-Royce Bristol Orpheus 101 turbojet. *Span:* 24 ft 0 in. (7·32 m). *Length (excluding probe):* 31 ft 9 in. (9·65 m). *Wing area:* 175·0 sq ft (16·26 sq m). *Normal take-off weight:* 8,250 lb (3,742 kg). *Maximum speed:* 635 mph (1,022 km/hr) at 35,000 ft (10,670 m). *Service ceiling:* 48,000 ft (14,600 m). *Maximum range (internal fuel):* 750 miles (1,200 km).

JAVELIN (U.K.)

48

Gloster Javelin F(AW). Mk 9 of the RAF (No 23 Squadron, Leuchars), *ca* 1963–64. *Engines:* Two 10,630/12,230 lb (4,822/5,547 kg) st Bristol Siddeley Sapphire 203/204 afterburning turbojets. *Span:* 52 ft 0 in. (15·85 m). *Length:* 56 ft 9 in. (17·30 m). *Wing area:* 927·0 sq ft (86·12 sq m). *Maximum take-off weight:* 42,930 lb (19,473 kg). *Maximum speed:* 684 mph (1,101 km/hr) at sea level. *Service ceiling:* 49,500 ft (15,087 m). *Maximum range with two auxiliary fuel tanks:* 930 miles (1,495 km).

SEA VIXEN (U.K.)

49

Hawker Siddeley Sea Vixen F(AW). Mk 2 of the Fleet Air Arm (Naval Air Fighter School, No 766 Squadron RNAS Yeovilton), 1967. *Engines:* Two 11,250 lb (5,103 kg) st Rolls-Royce Avon 208 turbojets. *Span:* 50 ft 0 in. (15·24 m). *Length:* 55 ft 7 in. (16·94 m). *Wing area:* 648·0 sq ft (60·20 sq m). *Take-off weight:* over 35,000 lb (15,876 kg). *Maximum speed:* approx 645 mph (1,038 km/hr) at 10,000 ft (3,050 m). *Service ceiling:* approx 48,000 ft (14,630 m). *Typical mission endurance:* 1 hr 30 min.

PHANTOM (U.S.A.)

50

McDonnell Douglas F-4B Phantom II of the US Navy (Squadron VF-84, USS *Independence*), *ca* 1961. *Engines:* Two 10,900/16,500 lb (4,944/7,484 kg) st General Electric J79-GE-8 afterburning turbojets. *Span:* 38 ft 5 in. (11·70 m). *Length:* 58 ft 3 in. (17·76 m). *Wing area:* 530·0 sq ft (49·24 sq m). *Maximum take-off weight:* 54,600 lb (24,766 kg). *Maximum speed:* 1,584 mph (2,550 km/hr) at 48,000 ft (14,630 m). *Combat ceiling:* 71,000 ft (21,640 m). *Typical radius with one external fuel tank:* over 900 miles (1,450 km).

PHANTOM (U.S.A.)

McDonnell Douglas F-4K Phantom FG. Mk I of the RAF (No 43 Squadron, Leuchars), 1969. *Engines:* Two 12,500/21,250 lb (5,670/9,638 kg) st Rolls-Royce Spey RB.168-25R Mk 201 afterburning turbofans. *Span:* 38 ft 5 in. (11·70 m). *Length:* 57 ft 11 in. (17·65 m). *Wing area:* 530·0 sq ft (49·24 sq m). *Maximum take-off weight:* 58,000 lb (26,308 kg). *Maximum speed:* 1,386 mph (2,230 km/hr) above 36,000 ft (11,000 m). *Typical tactical radius:* 550 miles (885 km).

AERITALIA (FIAT) G91 and G91Y (Italy)

52

Aeritalia (Fiat) G91T/1 of the Aeronautica Militare Italiano (Scuola Volo Basico Avanzato Aviogetti, Amendola), *ca* 1967. *Engine:* One 5,000 lb (2,268 kg) st Fiat-built Bristol Siddeley Orpheus 803 turbojet. *Span:* 28 ft 2½ in. (8·60 m). *Length:* 38 ft 4½ in. (11·70 m). *Wing area:* 176·7 sq ft (16·42 sq m). *Basic take-off weight:* 12,125 lb (5,500 kg). *Maximum speed:* 640 mph (1,030 km/hr) at 4,925 ft (1,500 m). *Service ceiling:* 39,375 ft (12,000 m). *Range:* 930 miles (1,500 km).

53

Aeritalia G91Y of the 8° Stormo Caccia-Bombardieri, Aeronautica Militare Italiano, 1973. *Engines:* Two 2,720/4,080 lb (1,235/1,850 kg) st General Electric J85-GE-13A afterburning turbojets. *Span:* 29 ft 6½ in. (9·01 m). *Length:* 38 ft 3½ in. (11·67 m). *Wing area:* 195·15 sq ft (18·13 sq m). *Maximum take-off weight:* 19,180 lb (8,700 kg). *Maximum speed:* 690 mph (1,110 km/hr) at sea level. *Service ceiling:* 41,000 ft (12,500 m). *Typical combat radius:* 372 miles (600 km) at sea level.

VOODOO (U.S.A.)

54

McDonnell CF-101B Voodoo of the Royal Canadian Air Force (No 416 Squadron, Air Defence Command), *ca* 1962. *Engines:* Two 11,990/14,880 lb (5,440/6,750 kg) st Pratt & Whitney J57-P-55 afterburning turbojets. *Span:* 39 ft 8 in. (12·09 m). *Length:* 67 ft 4¾ in. (20·54 m). *Wing area:* 638·0 sq ft (34·19 sq m). *Normal take-off weight:* 39,900 lb (18,098 kg). *Maximum speed:* 1,120 mph (1,802 km/hr) above 36,000 ft (11,000 m). *Service ceiling:* 52,000 ft (15,850 m). *Range on internal fuel:* 1,550 miles (2,495 km).

MARUT (India)

55

HAL HF-24 Marut Mk I of the Indian Air Force (probably No 10 Squadron), 1972. *Engines:* Two 4,850 lb (2,200 kg) st Rolls-Royce Bristol Orpheus 703 turbojets. *Span:* 29 ft 6¼ in. (9.00 m). *Length:* 52 ft 0¾ in. (15.87 m). *Wing area:* 306.8 sq ft (28.50 sq m). *Normal take-off weight:* 19,734 lb (8,951 kg). *Maximum speed:* 691 mph (1,112 km/hr) at sea level. *Service ceiling:* 45,925 ft (14,000 m). *Normal range:* 750 miles (1,210 km).

CRUSADER (U.S.A.)

56

Vought F-8E(FN) Crusader of the Aéronautique Navale (Flottille 12F, aircraft carrier *Clémenceau*), ca 1967. *Engine:* One 10,700/18,000 lb (4,853/8,165 kg) st Pratt & Whitney J57-P-20A afterburning turbojet. *Span:* 35 ft 2 in. (10·72 m). *Length:* 54 ft 6 in. (16·61 m). *Wing area:* 375·0 sq ft (34·84 sq m). *Maximum take-off weight:* 34,000 lb (15,422 kg). *Maximum speed:* 1,120 mph (1,802 km/hr) above 36,000 ft (11,000 m). *Service ceiling:* 58,000 ft (17,675 m). *Combat radius:* 600 miles (965 km).

CORSAIR (U.S.A.)

57

Vought A-7A Corsair II of the US Navy (Squadron VA-147, USS *Ranger*), Vietnam 1968. *Engine:* One 11,350 lb (5,150 kg) st Pratt & Whitney TF30-P-6 turbofan. *Span:* 38 ft 8¾ in. (11·80 m). *Length:* 46 ft 9 in. (14·25 m). *Wing area:* 375·0 sq ft (34·84 sq m). *Maximum catapult take-off weight:* 38,000 lb (17,237 kg). *Maximum speed:* 578 mph (930 km/hr) at sea level. *Typical tactical radius:* 810 miles (1,305 km).

LIGHTNING (U.K.)

58
BAC Lightning F. Mk 6 of the RAF (No 74 Squadron), *ca* 1968. *Engines:* Two 12,690/16,360 lb (5,756/7,420 kg) st Rolls-Royce Avon 301 afterburning turbojets. *Span:* 34 ft 10 in. (10·61 m). *Length (including probe):* 55 ft 3 in. (16·84 m). *Height:* 19 ft 7 in. (5·97 m). *Maximum take-off weight:* approx 48,000 lb (21,770 kg). *Maximum speed:* approx 1,450 mph (2,335 km/hr) above 36,000 ft (11,000 m). *Service ceiling:* over 60,000 ft (18,300 m). *Range with ventral tank:* approx 750 miles (1,200 km).

MIRAGE F1 (France)

59
Dassault Mirage F1-C of the 30e Escadre de Chasse (2/30 'Normandie-Niemen'), Armée de l'Air, early 1974. *Engine:* One 11,023/15,873 lb (5,000/7,200 kg) st SNECMA Atar 9K-50 afterburning turbojet. *Span:* 27 ft 6¾ in. (8·40 m). *Length:* 49 ft 2½ in. (15·00 m). *Wing area:* 269·1 sq ft (25·00 sq m). *Maximum take-off weight:* 33,510 lb (15,200 kg). *Maximum speed:* 1,450 mph (2,335 km/hr) above 36,000 ft (11,000 m). *Service ceiling:* 65,600 ft (20,000 m). *Maximum combat radius:* 745 miles (1,200 km).

MIRAGE G (France)

60

Dassault Mirage G-01 prototype in the insignia of the Armée de l'Air, 1969. *Engine:* One 11,686/20,500 lb (5,300/9,300 kg) st SNECMA-built Pratt & Whitney TF-306E afterburning turbofan. *Span (wings forward):* 42 ft 8 in. (13·00 m) *Span (wings swept):* approx 24 ft 3 in. (7·40 m). *Length:* 55 ft 1 in. (16·80 m). *Height:* 17 ft 6½ in. (5·35 m). *Maximum take-off weight:* 35,275 lb (16,000 kg). *Maximum speed:* 1,650 mph (2,655 km/hr) above 36,000 ft (11,000 m). *Service ceiling:* 65,600 ft (20,000 m). *Ferry range:* 4,000 miles (6,500 km).

JAGUAR (France/U.K.)

61

SEPECAT Jaguar GR. Mk 1 of the RAF Jaguar OCU at Lossiemouth, 1973. *Engines:* Two 5,115/7,304 lb (2,320/3,313 kg) st Rolls-Royce Turboméca Adour afterburning turbofans. *Span:* 28 ft 6 in. (8·69 m). *Length:* 50 ft 11 in. (15·52 m). *Wing area:* 258·3 sq ft (24·00 sq m). *Maximum take-off weight:* 34,000 lb (15,422 kg). *Maximum speed:* 990 mph (1,593 km/hr) above 36,000 ft (11,000 m). *Combat radius (high-low-high mission) on internal fuel:* 507 miles (815 km).

MITSUBISHI XT-2 (Japan)

Mitsubishi XT-2 second prototype in the insignia of the Japan Air Self-Defence Force, 1973. *Engines:* Two 4,400/7,140 lb (1,996/3,238 kg) st Rolls-Royce Turboméca Adour afterburning turbofans. *Span:* 25 ft 10 in. (7·87 m). *Length:* 58 ft 7 in. (17·86 m). *Wing area:* 228·0 sq ft (21·18 sq m). *Normal take-off weight:* 21,274 lb (9,650 kg) *Maximum speed:* 1,058 mph (1,703 km/hr) at 32,800 ft (10,000 m). *Service ceiling:* 50,025 ft (15,250 m). *Maximum (ferry) range with external tanks:* 1,785 miles (2,870 km).

THUNDERCHIEF (U.S.A.)

63

Republic F-105D Thunderchief of the US Air Force, Vietnam, *ca* 1967–68. *Engine:* One 17,200/26,500 lb (7,802/12,030 kg) st Pratt & Whitney J75-P-19W afterburning turbojet. *Span:* 34 ft 11¼ in. (10·65 m). *Length:* 67 ft 0¼ in. (20·43 m). *Wing area:* 385·0 sq ft (35·77 sq m). *Maximum take-off weight:* 52,546 lb (23,832 kg). *Maximum speed:* 1,388 mph (2,235 km/hr) above 36,000 ft (11,000 m). *Typical tactical radius:* 920 miles (1,480 km).

HARRIER (U.K.)

64

Hawker Siddeley Harrier GR. Mk 1 of the RAF, flown in the 1969 *Daily Mail* trans-Atlantic air race by Sqn Ldr T. Lecky-Thompson. *Engine:* One 19,000 lb (8,620 kg) st Rolls-Royce Bristol Pegasus Mk 101 vectored-thrust turbofan. *Span:* 25 ft 3 in. (7·70 m). *Length:* 45 ft 6 in. (13·87 m). *Wing area:* 201·1 sq ft (18·68 sq m). *Maximum take off weight:* over 25,000 lb (11,340 kg). *Maximum speed:* over 737 mph (1,186 km/hr) at low altitude. *Service ceiling:* over 50,000 ft (15,240 m). *Range with one in-flight refuelling:* over 3,455 miles (5,560 km).

DELTA DAGGER (U.S.A.)

65

Convair F-102A Delta Dagger of the US Air Forces Europe (525th Fighter Intercepter Squadron), *ca* 1962. *Engine:* One 11,700/17,200 lb (5,307/7,802 kg) st Pratt & Whitney J57-P-23 afterburning turbojet. *Span:* 38 ft 1½ in. (11·62 m). *Length (including nose probe):* 68 ft 4¾ in. (20·84 m). *Wing area:* 695·0 sq ft (64·57 sq m). *Normal take-off weight:* 27,700 lb (12,565 kg). *Maximum speed:* 825 mph (1,328 km/hr) above 36,000 ft (11,000 m). *Service ceiling:* 54,000 ft (16,460 m). *Range with underwing tanks:* 1,350 miles (2,175 km).

DELTA DART (U.S.A.)

66

General Dynamics (Convair) F-106A Delta Dart of the US Air Force (94th Fighter Intercepter Squadron, Air Defense Command), *ca* 1963. *Engine:* One 17,200/24,500 lb (7,802/11,113 kg) st Pratt & Whitney J75-P-17 afterburning turbojet. *Span:* 38 ft 3½ in. (11·67 m). *Length (including nose probe):* 70 ft 8¾ in. (21·56 m). *Wing area:* 697·8 sq ft (63·83 sq m). *Normal take-off weight:* 35,500 lb (16,103 kg). *Maximum speed:* 1,525 mph (2,455 km/hr) above 36,000 ft (11,000 m). *Service ceiling:* 57,000 ft (17,375 m). *Combat radius, standard fuel:* 575 miles (925 km).

DRAKEN (Sweden)

Saab J 35F Draken of the Flygvapnet (F13 Wing, Norrköping), 1969. *Engine:* One 12,790/17,650 lb (5,800/8,000 kg) st Rolls-Royce/Volvo Flygmotor RM6C afterburning turbojet. *Span:* 30 ft 10 in. (9·40 m). *Length:* 50 ft 4 in. (15·35 m). *Wing area:* 529·6 sq ft (49·20 sq m). *Maximum take-off weight:* 33,070 lb (15,000 kg). *Maximum speed:* 1,320 mph (2,125 km/hr) at 39,375 ft (12,000 m). *Service ceiling:* 49,200 ft (15,000 m). *Typical radius with two 1,000 lb bombs and two drop-tanks:* 623 miles (1,003 km).

VIGGEN (Sweden)

68

Saab AJ 37 Viggen of the Flygvapnet (F7 Wing, Såtenäs), 1972. *Engine:* One 14,770/26,450 lb (6,700/12,000 kg) st Volvo Flygmotor RM8A afterburning turbofan. *Span:* 34 ft 9¼ in. (10·60 m). *Length (incl probe):* 53 ft 5¾ in. (16·30 m). *Wing area:* 495·1 sq ft (46·00 sq m). *Take-off weight (normal armament):* approx 35,275 lb (16,000 kg). *Maximum speed:* 1,320 mph (2,125 km/hr) at 39,375 ft (12,000 m). *Tactical radius with external armament:* 620 miles (1,000 km).

MIRAGE III (France)

69

Dassault Mirage III-S of the Schweizerische Flugwaffe, *ca* 1968. *Engine:* One 9,430/13,670 lb (4,280/6,200 kg) st SNECMA Atar 9C afterburning turbojet. *Span:* 27 ft 0 in. (8·22 m). *Length (incl probe):* 49 ft 3½ in. (15·03 m). *Wing area:* 375·1 sq ft (34·85 sq m). *Maximum take-off weight:* 29,760 lb (13,500 kg). *Maximum speed:* 1,460 mph (2,350 km/hr) at 39,375 ft (12,000 m). *Service ceiling:* 55,775 ft (17,000 m). *Typical combat radius:* 180 miles (290 km).

MIRAGE III (France)

70

Dassault Mirage III-R of the 3rd Escadron, 33rd Escadre, Armée de l'Air, Strasbourg ca 1966-67. *Length (incl probe):* 50 ft 10¼ in. (15·50 m). *Wing area:* 375·1 sq ft (34·85 sq m). *Typical radius:* 745 miles (1,200 km). *Other data as for Mirage III-S.*

MIRAGE 5 (France)

71

Dassault Mirage 5-BA of the 2e Wing, Force Aérienne Belge, Florennes, 1972. *Length:* 51 ft 0¼ in. (15·55 m). *Combat radius with 2,000 lb (907 kg) bomb load:* 808 miles (1,300 km). *Other data as for Mirage III-S.*

MiG-21 (U.S.S.R.)

72

Mikoyan MiG-21F (Fishbed-C) of the Cuban Fuerza Aérea Revolucionaria, ca 1967. *Engine:* One 9,480/12,676 lb (4,300/5,750 kg) st Tumansky RD-11 afterburning turbojet. *Span:* 23 ft 5½ in. (7·15 m). *Length (excluding nose probe):* 44 ft 2 in. (13·46 m). *Wing area:* 247·6 sq ft (23·00 sq m). *Normal take-off weight:* approx 16,700 lb (7,575 kg). *Maximum speed:* approx 1,320 mph (2,125 km/hr) at 36,000 ft (11,000 m). *Service ceiling:* approx 64,000 ft (21,000 m). *Combat radius (clean):* 375 miles (600 km).

73

MiG-21UTI Mongol-B (Type 66 Series 600) of the Indian Air Force, 1973. *Data generally similar to those for MiG-21MF.*

MiG-21 (U.S.S.R.)

74

Mikoyan MiG-21MF (Fishbed-K) of the Polskie Lotnictwo Wojskowe, 1973. *Engine:* One 11,244/14,550 lb (5,100/6,600 kg) st Tumansky RD-13-300 afterburning turbojet; provision for two JATO rockets giving additional 6,614 lb (3,000 kg) st for take-off. *Span, Length and Wing area:* As for MiG-21F. *Maximum take-off weight:* approx 20,725 lb (9,400 kg). *Maximum speed:* 1,385 mph (2,230 km/hr) above 36,000 ft (11,000 m). *Combat radius:* 350 miles (560 km).

SUKHOI Su-9 (U.S.S.R.)

75

Sukhoi Su-9 (Fishpot-B) of the Soviet Air Force (IA-PVO) *ca* 1964. *Engine:* One 15,432/19,842 lb (7,000/9,000 kg) st Lyulka AL-7F afterburning turbojet. *Span:* 26 ft 0 in. (7·90 m). *Length (including nose probe):* 56 ft 0 in. (17·00 m). *Wing area:* 269·0 sq ft (25·00 sq m). *Normal take-off weight:* 26,455 lb (12,000 kg). *Maximum speed:* 1,190 mph (1,915 km/hr) above 36,000 ft (11,000 m). *Service ceiling:* 55,775 ft (17,000 m). *All data estimated.*

SUKHOI Su-15 (U.S.S.R.)

76

Sukhoi Su-15 (Flagon-A) in Soviet Air Force markings, as displayed at Domodedovo, 1967. *Engines:* Two 22,046 lb (10,000 kg) st Lyulka afterburning turbojets. *Span:* 33 ft 3½ in. (10·15 m). *Length:* 68 ft 0 in. (20·75 m). *Height:* 16 ft 5 in. (5·00 m). *Normal take-off weight:* 35,275 lb (16,000 kg). *Maximum speed:* 1,650 mph (2,655 km/hr) above 36,000 ft (11,000 m). *Combat radius:* 450 miles (725 km). *All data estimated.*

YAKOVLEV Yak-28P (U.S.S.R.)

Yakovlev Yak-28P (Firebar) of the Soviet Air Force, *ca* 1971. *Engines:* Two 9,480/13,120 lb (4,300/5,950 kg) st Tumansky RD-11 afterburning turbojets. *Span:* 42 ft 6 in. (12·95 m). *Length:* 74 ft 7¾ in. (22·75 m). *Wing area:* 410·0 sq ft (38·00 sq m). *Maximum take-off weight:* 35,275 lb (16,000 kg). *Maximum speed:* 733 mph (1,180 km/hr) above 36,000 ft (11,000 m). *Service ceiling:* 55,120 ft (16,800 m). *Maximum combat radius:* 575 miles (925 km). *All data estimated.*

TUPOLEV Tu-28 (U.S.S.R.)

78

Tupolev Tu-28P (Fiddler) of the Soviet Air Force, *ca* 1968. *Engines:* Two 27,560 lb (12,250 kg) st afterburning turbojets of unknown type. *Span:* 65 ft 6 in. (18·30 m). *Length:* 85 ft 3½ in. (27·40 m). *Wing area:* 840·0 sq ft (78·00 sq m). *Maximum take-off weight:* 99,200 lb (45,000 kg). *Maximum speed:* 1,120 mph (1,800 km/hr) at 39,375 ft (12,000 m). *Service ceiling:* 64,000 ft (19,500 m). *Typical radius:* 745 miles (1,200 km). *All data estimated.*

MiG-25 (U.S.S.R.)

79

Mikoyan MiG-25 (Foxbat-B) in Soviet Air Force markings, *ca* 1972. *Engines:* Two 24,250 lb (11,000 kg) st Tumansky afterburning turbojets. *Span:* 41 ft 0 in. (12·50 m). *Length:* 73 ft 9¾ in. (22·50 m). *Height:* 13 ft 7½ in. (4·15 m). *Maximum take-off weight:* 64,200 lb (29,120 kg). *Maximum speed:* 1,980 mph (3,185 km/hr) at 60,000 ft (18,300 m). *Service ceiling:* 78,740 ft (24,000 m). *Maximum range:* 1,620 miles (2,600 km). *All data estimated.*

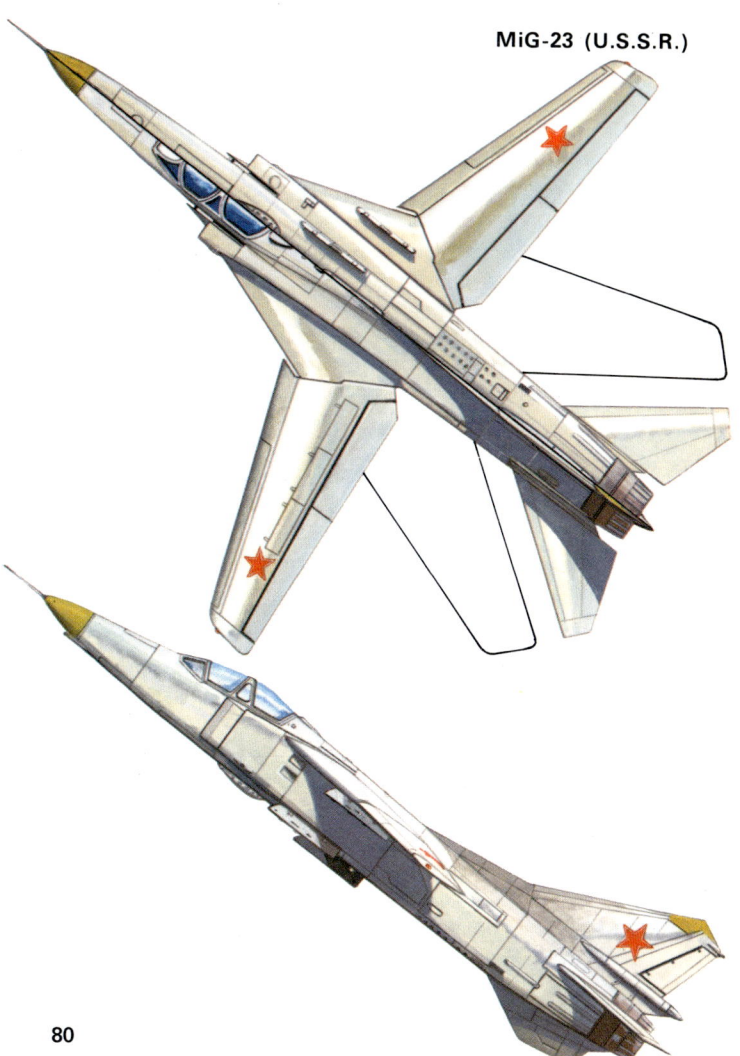

MiG-23 (U.S.S.R.)

Mikoyan MiG-23U in Soviet Air Force markings, *ca* 1972–73. *Engine:* One 14,330/20,500 lb (6,500/9,300 kg) st afterburning turbojet of unknown type. *Span (wings forward):* 44 ft 11½ in. (13·70 m). *Span (wings swept):* 26 ft 1 in. (7·95 m). *Length:* 55 ft 1½ in. (16·80 m). *Height:* 13 ft 1½ in. (4·00 m). *Maximum take-off weight:* 33,070 lb (15,000 kg). *Maximum speed:* 1,520 mph (2,445 km/hr) above 36,000 ft (11,000 m). *Service ceiling:* 59,000 ft (18,000 m). *Combat radius:* 600 miles (960 km). *All data estimated.*

GENERAL DYNAMICS F-111 (U.S.A.)

81

General Dynamics F-111A of the US Air Force (Tactical Air Command), *ca* 1967. *Engines:* Two 12,500/21,000 lb (5,670/9,525 kg) st Pratt & Whitney TF30-P-3 afterburning turbofans. *Span (wings forward):* 63 ft 0 in. (19·20 m). *Span (wings swept):* 31 ft 11½ in. (9·74 m). *Length:* 73 ft 6 in. (22·40 m). *Height:* 17 ft 1½ in. (5·22 m). *Maximum take-off weight:* 91,500 lb (41,504 kg). *Maximum speed:* 1,650 mph (2,655 km/hr) above 36,000 ft (11,000 m). *Service ceiling:* over 60,000 ft (18,300 m). *Maximum range on internal fuel:* over 3,800 miles (6,100 km).

TOMCAT (U.S.A.)

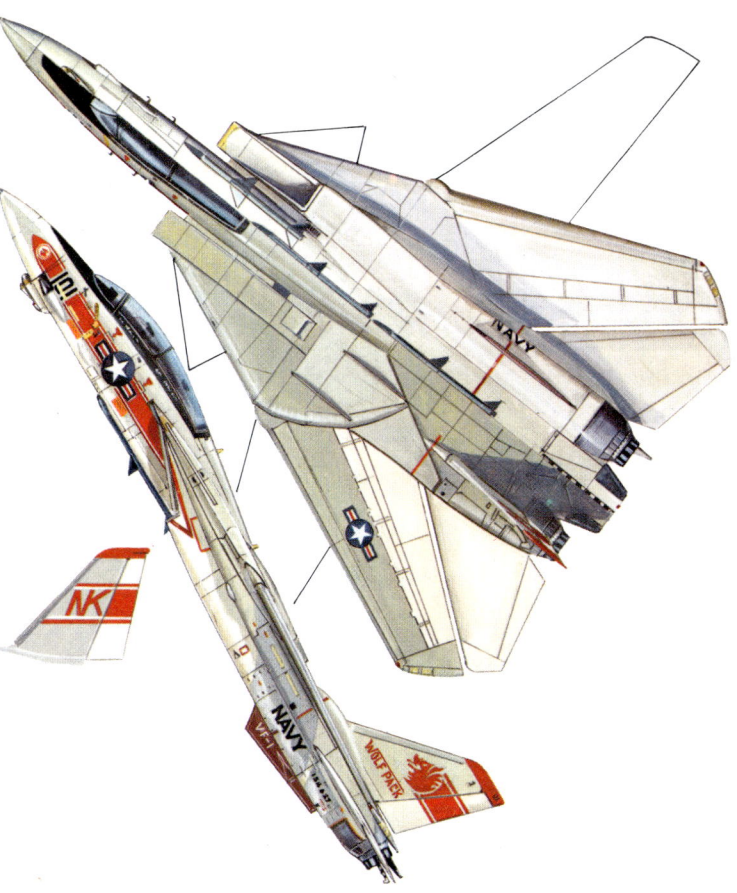

82

Grumman F-14A Tomcat of Squadron VF-1, US Naval Air Station Miramar, California, 1973. *Engines:* Two 20,900 lb (9,480 kg) st Pratt & Whitney TF30-P-412A afterburning turbofans. *Span (wings forward):* 64 ft 1½ in. (19·54 m). *Span (wings swept):* 38 ft 1·9 in. (11·63 m). *Length:* 61 ft 11·9 in. (18·89 m) *Wing area:* 565·0 sq ft (52·49 sq m). *Maximum take-off weight:* 68,567 lb (31,101 kg). *Maximum speed:* over 1,450 mph (2,333 km/hr) above 36,000 ft (11,000 m). *Service ceiling:* above 56,000 ft (17,070 m). *Typical combat radius:* 450 miles (724 km).

EAGLE (U.S.A.)

McDonnell Douglas F-15A Eagle, development aircraft, 1973. *Engines:* Two approx 25,000 lb (11,340 kg) st Pratt & Whitney F100-PW-101 afterburning turbofans. *Span:* 42 ft 9¾ in. (13·05 m). *Length:* 63 ft 9¾ in. (19·45 m). *Wing area:* 608·0 sq ft (56·48 sq m). *Maximum take-off weight (interceptor):* 40,000 lb (18,143 kg). *Maximum speed:* more than 1,650 mph (2,655 km/hr) above 36,000 ft (11,000 m). *Absolute ceiling:* 66,900 ft (20,390 m). *Ferry range (three drop-tanks):* more than 2,880 miles (4,635 km).

DOMINIE (U.K.)

84

Hawker Siddeley Dominie T. Mk 1 of the RAF (No 1 Air Navigation School, Stradishall), *ca* spring 1966. *Engines:* Two 3,000 lb (1,360 kg) st Rolls-Royce Bristol Viper 520 turbojets. *Span:* 47 ft 0 in. (14·33 m). *Length:* 47 ft 5 in. (14·45 m). *Wing area:* 353·0 sq ft (32·80 sq m). *Maximum take-off weight:* 21,200 lb (9,615 kg). *Maximum cruising speed:* 500 mph (805 km/hr) at 30,000 ft (9,145 m). *Service ceiling:* 40,000 ft (12,200 m). *Range with standard fuel:* 1,700 miles (2,736 km).

SABRELINER (U.S.A.)

85

Rockwell (North American) T-39A Sabreliner of the US Air Force (Air Training Command), *ca* 1962. *Engines:* Two 3,000 lb (1,361 kg) st Pratt & Whitney J60-P-3A turbojets. *Span:* 44 ft 5¼ in. (13·54 m). *Length:* 43 ft 9 in. (13·34 m). *Wing area:* 342·05 sq ft (31·78 sq m). *Maximum take-off weight:* 17,760 lb (8,056 kg). *Maximum speed:* 540 mph (869 km/hr) at 36,000 ft (11,000 m). *Service ceiling:* 39,000 ft (11,890 m). *Maximum range:* 1,950 miles (3,140 km).

1 **Cessna T-41 Mescalero**
By the beginning of 1970 more than sixteen thousand members of the Cessna 172/Skyhawk family of lightplanes had been built. By far the greater proportion of these were for the civil market, but the type has also been adopted in some numbers by several air forces for pre-selection and primary training. The Cessna Model 172, as described in *Private Aircraft since 1946*, is a descendant of the Model 120 of 1945, and itself appeared some ten years later. First military order was placed by the U.S. Air Force, which in July 1964 ordered a hundred and seventy Cessna 172s 'off the shelf' as T-41A basic trainers. Delivery of these had been made by July 1965, and U.S.A.F. trainee pilots undergo about 30 hours on this type (at commercial flying schools operating under government contract) before graduating to another Cessna type, the T-37B primary jet trainer. Additional orders covered a further thirty-four T-41As for the U.S.A.F., twenty-five for the Fuerza Aérea del Peru and eight for the Fuerza Aérea Ecuatoriana. About forty of this version have also been supplied to the Hellenic Air Force. Another large order, this time for the more powerful Model R172E (210 h.p. Continental IO-360-D engine with fuel injection), was placed in August 1966 by the U.S. Army, which purchased two hundred and fifty-five with the designation T-41B. These had all been delivered by March 1967, and in October of that year forty-five T-41Cs (with fixed-pitch propellers) were ordered by the U.S. Air Force; this total was later increased to fifty-two. Columbia ordered thirty T-41Ds, and Ecuador twelve, which have constant-speed propellers and a different electrical system but are otherwise similar. Model 172s also serve with the air forces of Bolivia (three or more), Saudi Arabia (eight) and Singapore (eight).

The Model 172 is not the only single-engined high-wing type of Cessna lightplane in military service. Others include the Model 180 (230 h.p. Continental O-470-R), Model 182 and Model 185/U-17 Skywagon (260 h.p. IO-470-F engine), which are in service with the air arms of Argentina, Australia, Bolivia, Burma, Canada, Chile, Ecuador, Greece, Guatemala, Honduras, Indonesia, Jamaica, South Korea, Laos, Mexico, Nicaragua, Paraguay, Peru, South Africa, Turkey, Uruguay and South Vietnam.

2 **Dornier Do 27**
This useful little aeroplane is a true 'general purpose' type, and it might with equal justification have been included in the companion volume

as a transport aircraft. Seating from six to eight people, it may be used for observation, liaison, casualty evacuation and utility transport roles; and a substantial number have been built for the civil market. It is, however, as a training aircraft that its chief military use lies, and of the six hundred and eighty Do 27s built, four hundred and twenty-eight were for the Federal German armed forces as training and liaison aircraft. The Schweizerische Flugwaffe had ten for utility roles, the Nigerian Air Force ten (later increased) for training; other forces to have employed the Do 27 include those of Belgium, Nigeria, Portugal, South Africa (no longer in service), Sweden, Turkey and Zaïre. Fifty were built under licence in Spain, for the Ejército del Aire, as the CASA C.127, and in fact it was in Spain that the aeroplane had its origins, in the Do 25 which was powered by a 150 h.p. ENMA Tigre G-IVB and flown for the first time on 25 June 1954. The prototype Do 27 was also begun in Spain, but the parts were then taken to Germany for assembly prior to the first flight on 27 June 1955. Altogether, three Do 27 prototypes were completed; series production in Germany began in the following year and ended in 1966, at which time six hundred and twenty had been built. The production facility was, however, kept open, and a further sixty aircraft were subsequently completed. Most military examples are Do 27As or Do 27Bs, basically similar but with dual controls in the B model for pilot training.

3 Soko P-2 Kraguj

Notwithstanding the remarkable capability of small jet aircraft to carry impressive loads of weapons beneath the wings and fuselage, there have in post-war years been recurring instances of the usefulness of even smaller, piston-engined aircraft carrying more modest weapon loads for use in local or 'brushfire' engagements. The concept was pioneered in the early 1950s by a U.S. design, the Fletcher Defender, potentially an excellent coin (counter-insurgency) type but rejected, in those pre-Vietnam days, because it did not fulfil an existing requirement. Among more recent resurrections of the concept, one of the most interesting types to appear is the little single-seat Kraguj, designed at the Aeronautical Research Establishment at Beograd, produced by the Soko factory at Mostar in Yugoslavia and first flown in prototype form in 1966. Of simple, all-metal construction, it can take off and land using grass fields or unprepared airstrips of less than 395 ft. (120 m.), and can be flown by pilots with only a minimum of training hours behind them. The Kraguj has a fixed armament of one 7·7 mm. machine-gun in each wing outboard of the propeller disc, with 650 r.p.g., and there are six underwing attachment points for weapons. Of these, the two inboard points can each carry a cluster of small bombs, a single bomb of up to 100 kg., a 40 U.S. gallon (150 litre) napalm canister or a pod of twelve rockets. The four outboard points can each carry a single 57 mm. or 127 mm. air-to-ground rocket. The Kraguj entered production and service in 1968, and about thirty were built for ground attack units of the Yugoslav Air Force.

4 Scottish Aviation Bulldog

Development of the Bulldog was initiated in 1968 by the former Beagle Aircraft Ltd. as the B.125 Series 1, a military trainer based on the Beagle Pup. Beagle completed the first prototype (G-AXEH), which flew for the first time on 19 May 1969, and at the time of the company's collapse in early 1970 had begun construction of a second aircraft, G-AXIG. This was taken over and completed by Scottish Aviation, making its first flight on 14 February 1971. Scottish Aviation also took over responsibility for the initial production order, placed earlier with Beagle by the Swedish government, for seventy-eight Bulldog Series 100 (Model 101). Designated SK 61 in Sweden, they were delivered to the Air Force (fifty-eight) and Army (twenty), following the first flight of a production Bulldog on 22 June 1971. A further twenty Series 100s were built, these comprising fifteen Model 102s for the Royal Malaysian Air Force and five Model 103s for the Kenya Air Force. Production then switched to the generally similar Series 120, initially to meet an R.A.F. order for one hundred and thirty Model 121 Bulldogs which are intended primarily for service with University Air Squadrons. The R.A.F. designation is T. Mk 1; the first of these (XX513) was flown for the first time on 30 January 1973, and the Bulldog entered R.A.F. service with No. 2 F.T.S. at Church Fenton later that year. Subsequent orders include six Model 122s for the Ghana Air Force (all delivered), twenty Model 123s for the Nigerian Air Force (first deliveries January 1974), and five Model 125s for the Jordan Royal Academy of Aeronautics (also for 1974 delivery). The designation Model 124 covers a Scottish Aviation demonstrator (G-ASAL) fitted with four underwing hardpoints for up to 640 lb. (290 kg.) of light attack weapons. The Bulldog is basically a 2-seater, but an optional third seat may be fitted at the rear. The various models differ primarily in the customer equipment fitted; the Series 120 is generally similar to the Series 100 except for increased structural strength, for aerobatic flying, and an improved instrument panel.

5 Beechcraft T-34 Mentor

The Beechcraft Model 45 Mentor was evolved from the butterfly-tailed Bonanza lightplane to provide a piston-engined basic trainer for the U.S. Air Force and Navy. The first private-venture prototype (N8591A) made its first flight on 2 December 1948, powered by a 205 h.p. Continental E-185-8 engine, and three YT-34s were evaluated by the U.S.A.F. in 1950.

Subsequently more than twelve hundred Mentors were built, in the U.S.A., Argentina, Canada and Japan. Beginning in October 1953 the U.S. Air Force took delivery of four hundred and fifty T-34As (a hundred of these being built in Canada by CCF, which also completed twenty-five Model A45s for the R.C.A.F.), and the U.S. Navy received four hundred and twenty-three of the essentially similar T-34B. Neither service has for some time used the Mentor for training, but the Beech two-seater was still current equipment with several foreign air arms in 1974. Twenty-three former R.C.A.F. Mentors were transferred to the Türk Hava Kuvvetleri, and one to the Hellenic Air Force; Fuji in Japan built or assembled a hundred and forty for the J.A.S.D.F. and thirty-six for the Philippine Air Force; and FMA in Argentina completed seventy-five for the Fuerza Aérea Argentina during 1956-62. Forty-one Model B45s were supplied by Beech to the Fuerzas Aéreas Venezolanas; sixty-six to the Fuerza Aérea de Chile; three to the Fuerza Aérea Salvadorena; forty-one to the Fuerza Aérea Colombiana; four to the Aviación Naval Mexicana; and fifteen to the Fuerza Aérea Argentina. Others were supplied by the U.S.A.F. to the air forces of Saudi Arabia and Spain. Mentors are also in service in Ecuador, Indonesia and Uruguay.

In Japan, Fuji produced a number of developed versions of the Mentor, the first of these being the LM-1 Nikko, of which twenty-seven were supplied to the J.G.S.D.F. as multi-purpose liaison aircraft. A more powerful 4/5-seat version, with a 340 h.p. Lycoming IGSO-480 engine, was designated LM-2: two examples were produced by conversion of LM-1 airframes. A prototype known as the KM, with similar powerplant, was flown in December 1958, and from this Fuji developed the KM-2, a 2/4-seat side-by-side intermediate trainer of which the first example was flown on 16 July 1962. Twenty-five KM-2s were built initially for the J.M.S.D.F., delivery of these taking place between September 1962 and May 1965; three additional examples were ordered in 1968, and a further three in 1974. On 21 September 1973 Beech flew the first of two YT-34Cs, to evaluate a possible upgrading of the Mentor by installing a 715 s.h.p. United Aircraft of Canada PT6A-25 turboprop engine. This programme was continuing in 1974.

6 **North American T-28 Trojan**

Having started out as a basic trainer to replace the veteran Texan—no mean ambition in itself – the T-28 (the first of two XT-28s was flown on 26 September 1949) stayed to become an operational warplane which, in the early part of the war in Vietnam, proved more effective for 'brushfire' warfare than many of its supersonic and heavily automated companions. As a trainer the T-28 was superseded in the U.S.A. in the late 1950s by the T-37, after one thousand one hundred and ninety-four T-28As, four hundred and eighty-nine U.S. Navy T-28Bs and two hundred and ninety-nine Navy T-28Cs had been built up to 1953. The Navy models were fitted with 1,425 h.p. R-1820-86 engines. Many T-28A/B/Cs were later sold to foreign air forces, including those of Argentina, Bolivia, the Congo, Cuba, Ecuador, Ethiopia, Japan, Mexico, the Republic of Korea and the Philippines.

In addition, from 1962–68 three hundred and twenty-one T-28As were converted to T-28Ds by North American, and a further seventy-two in 1970 and others in 1973 by Fairchild, chiefly for the South Vietnamese and Royal Thai Air Forces. The T-28D, strengthened structurally and with a 1,425 h.p. Wright R-1820-56S engine, has six underwing stores points; the inner pair generally carry a machine-gun pod apiece, the others a variety of bombs, napalm tanks or rockets. One hundred and sixty T-28Ds, with ammunitition housed in the wings, were designated T-28D-5. A North American licence was granted to the PacAero Corporation to build an export conversion known as the T-28-R Nomad: six of these went to the Brazilian Navy, and the Nomad was also evaluated in France, where two hundred and forty-five were converted under sub-licence by Sud-Aviation. The French-built version, known as the Fennec, was used by the Armée de l'Air in Algeria. The first of three YAT-28Es was flown on 15 February 1963, and these were evaluated during 1964–66, but this model did not go into production. The YAT-28E was an experimental counter-insurgency version with a taller fin and rudder, a 2,445 s.h.p. Lycoming T55 turboprop engine, and extra stores points for a total load of 4,000 lb (1,814 kg.).

7 **Yakovlev Yak-18 ('Max')**
Design of the Yak-18 was initiated by the Yakovlev design bureau in 1938 under the pre-war designation AIR-19 as a successor to the widely-used UT-2 (also of Yakovlev origin) which was then the standard Soviet military and civil flying school trainer. The design was resurrected after World War 2, and under the new designation Yak-18 a prototype was completed and flown in the summer of 1945. With a 125 h.p. M-11D radial engine and fixed landing gear, this was considered below the performance standard required, and a second prototype was built in 1946 with retractable gear and a 160 h.p. M-11FR engine. This machine still had a somewhat dated appearance, due chiefly to the old-fashioned 'helmet' fairings over the engine cylinders, but it was strongly built, had a well-equipped cockpit and was easy to fly; and its performance was of a high order. Accordingly, this initial version of the Yak-18 entered production and was delivered to Soviet Air Force and civilian flying schools and clubs in considerable numbers from 1947. It remained in produc-

tion until 1955, when it was superseded by the Yak-18U with an improved (but still helmeted) cowling, a 1 ft. 6 in. (0·46 m.) longer nose, tricycle landing gear and increased take-off weight. Performance of the Yak-18U was noticeably inferior to that of the original version, but it proved to be only an interim model pending availability of the Yak-18A which entered production in 1956–57. This retained the nosewheel undercarriage, had 1 ft. 0 in. (0·30 m.) greater wing span, a further 1 ft. 6 in. increase in overall length and a small, curved fillet between the fin leading-edge and fuselage. The major improvement introduced by the Yak-18A, however, was the installation of a 260 h.p. Ivchenko AI-14R radial engine in a clean, cylindrical cowling, which gave the aircraft a much-enhanced performance. Two production models were built: one with the main landing gear retracting forwards, but not fully, and the other with the gear retracting inwards to lie completely buried within the wings. The Yak-18, -18U and -18A, all 2-seat aircraft, are known collectively by the N.A.T.O. code name 'Max'. In 1974 the Yak-18 and -18A were still in extensive use by the air forces of Afghanistan, Albania, Bulgaria, China, Egypt, East Germany, Hungary, North Korea, Mali, Mongolia, Romania, the Soviet Union and North Vietnam. Single-seat aerobatic and advanced training versions, designated Yak-18P and -18M and code-named 'Mouse', have also appeared but have been built mostly for civil organisations; they do not appear to have entered military service on any scale. Total Yak-18 production (all variants) is thought to have been in the region of six thousand eight hundred aircraft.

8 Yakovlev Yak-11 ('Moose')

Alexander Yakovlev has over many years established himself not only as a prolific designer of aeroplanes but also as one of the most creative. The range of Yakovlev products in the past thirty years has included trainers, fighters, all-weather interceptors, reconnaissance aircraft and helicopters, ranging in complexity from the little Yak-18 basic trainer to the Yak-28 'Brewer' tactical strike aircraft. One Yakovlev aircraft which has been in widespread service for some twenty-five years is the Yak-11, an aeroplane which is appealing both aesthetically and aerodynamically and which still fulfils the function of intermediate pilot training in almost a score of air forces. Its two seats are placed in tandem under a long 'greenhouse' canopy, the instructor occupying the rear seat. For armament training duties it mounts a 7·7 mm. machine-gun in the port side of the upper engine cowling, and there are two underwing shackles for the carriage of practice bombs. The Yak-11, which has justifiably been dubbed 'the Russian Harvard', was based largely on the wartime Yak-9 fighter. It began to join Soviet Air Force training units in 1947, and since that time several thousand have gone into service, many of these being the Czechoslovak licence-built version, which is known as the C.11. The Yak-11 still served in 1974 with the air forces of Afghanistan, Albania, Algeria, Bulgaria, China, Czechoslovakia, East Germany, Egypt, Hungary, Iraq, North Korea, Mongolia, Romania, Somalia, Syria, the U.S.S.R., North Vietnam and the Yemen.

9 Piaggio P. 149D

In 1951 the Italian Air Force selected two new piston-engined primary training aircraft: the Dutch Fokker S.11 Instructor (built under licence by Macchi as the M.416) and the Piaggio P.148 designed by Ing C. P. Casiraghi. The latter, first flown on 12 February 1951, was a side-by-side 2/3-seat aircraft with a 190 h.p. Lycoming O-435-A engine and non-retractable tailwheel landing gear. One hundred were built for the Italian Air Force. From it was developed the 4/5-seat P.149, which had a similar-sized airframe incorporating an enlarged cabin, more powerful engine and retractable tricycle undercarriage. The first of two P.149 prototypes (MM 559), powered by a 260 h.p. GO-435 Lycoming engine, was flown for the first time on 19 June 1953; these and the production aircraft (GO-480 engine) had many structural components in common with the P.148. Intended originally as a 4-seat tourer or 2-seat aerobatic aircraft, the P.149 was selected in 1955 for 4/5-seat liaison and 2-seat basic training duties by the Federal German Luftwaffe, which ordered seventy-two from the Italian company. These were delivered (the first aircraft being AS+401) from April 1957. A further one hundred and ninety were built or assembled in Germany under licence by Focke-Wulf; these were delivered to the Luftwaffe from November 1957, production being completed in 1959. German designation of the aircraft is P.149D. They have been replaced in the liaison role by the Dornier Do 27, but about a hundred trainers were still in German military service at the end of the 1960s, together with about thirty civil-registered examples. In 1965 Germany supplied twenty-six P.149Ds to the Nigerian Air Force, which utilised them for armament training; smaller batches are or were operated by the air forces of Somalia, Tanzania, Uganda and Zaïre.

10 SIAI-Marchetti SF.260MX and SF.260W

Said to be one of the best to handle among current light aircraft, the SF.260MX had its origins in the civil F.250 prototype designed in Italy by Dott Ing Stelio Frati, built by Aviamilano, and flown for the first time on 15 July 1964, powered by a 250 h.p. Lycoming O-540-A1D5 engine. The F.250 was later put into production for the civil market, with a more powerful engine, by SIAI-Marchetti as the SF.260. In this market it has been quite successful, SIAI-Marchetti being well into its second batch of fifty production aircraft by 1974. Among earlier customers was Sabena, which purchased thirteen for its Ecole de l'Aviation Civile at Grimbergen, and this was no doubt an influencing factor in the emergence of a military trainer version, for which Belgium was the first (and, up to 1974, still the largest) customer. Thirty-six SF.260Ms were ordered by the Force Aérienne Belge, the first military trainer making its first flight on 10 October 1970. The general export designation SF.260MX was then applied to this version, the X being replaced, for aircraft ordered, by a letter indicating the individual customers. Up to late-1974 these included the air forces of Dubai (one), Italy (twenty-five SF.260 AMI), Morocco (two), the Philippines (thirty-two SF.260 MP), Singapore (sixteen SF.260 MS), Thailand (twelve SF.260 MT), Zaïre (twelve SF.260MC) and Zambia (eight SF.260MZ); more than half of these had by then been delivered. A fully-aerobatic 3-seater, the SF.260MX is intended basically for flying rather than armament training, but a 2-seat SF.260W armed version is also available. (The W stood originally for Warrior, a name later dropped to avoid confusion with the Piper Cherokee Warrior.) The SF.260W, which first flew in May 1972, has two underwing hardpoints, these permitting the carriage of two 50 kg. bombs (120 kg. if flown as a single-seater); two Matra 7·62 mm. machine-gun pods; two pods each containing either six 68 mm. SNEB, nine 2·75 in. FFAR or eighteen 2 in. rockets; or two cartridge throwers. Sixteen SF.260Ws have been ordered by the Philippine Air Force and twelve by the Tunisian Air Force.

11 **FMA I.A.35 Huanquero and I.A.50 GII**

A product of Argentina's only constructor of military aircraft, the Fábrica Militar de Aviones at Córdoba, the I.A. 35 Huanquero is a nationally-evolved multi-purpose aeroplane built in quantity for the Fuerza Aérea Argentina. The prototype, originally named *Justicialista del Aire*, was renamed Huanquero after the downfall of the Perón government. When it made its first flight on 7 September 1953, its twin 650 h.p. I.A.R.-19A El Indio radial engines were also being flown for the first time. Series production, to meet orders for a hundred aircraft, was to have begun in 1955, but was deferred until two years later, the first production aircraft flying on 27 March 1957. Thirty-one Huanqueros had been built by 1962, and production was completed by early 1965. Aircraft manufactured from 1959 onward were fitted with 840 h.p. I.A.R.-19C engines. Four basic versions of the Huanquero were built, and were still in service in the early 1970s. At that time Air Brigade I had the I.A. 35-II light transport version, which has a crew of three; seats are provided for seven passengers, and external cargo panniers may also be fitted.

The much-modified original prototype was also brought up to similar standard and placed in service with Air Brigade I. The 1st Photographic Squadron of Air Brigade II uses the I.A.35-IV for photographic and general reconnaissance duties; the I.A.35-Ia aircrew trainer and the I.A.35-Ib bombing and gunnery trainer/ground-attack version serves with Air Brigades IV and V and Attack and Exploration Groups I and II. The I.A.35-Ia normally carries a flight crew of three, four pupils and an instructor, and is used for the training of pilots, navigators and photographers. Operational equipment of the I.A.35-Ib includes two fixed, forward-firing 7·65 mm. machine-guns, two similar guns in a hydraulically-operated dorsal turret, an MK.14 bomb sight and underwing racks for four 50 kg. or two 100 kg. bombs and two 5 in. or eight 2·25 in. rockets. The I.A.35-III was a projected ambulance version, accommodating four stretcher cases with an accompanying medical attendant, but was not built. From the basic design a commercial version with twin Bastan turboprop engines was evolved as the Guarani I. This was further developed and extensively re-designed as the single-finned Guarani II (now GII); it flew for the first time on 23 April 1963 and is described in the companion *Bombers* volume.

12 FMA I.A.58 Pucará

At the beginning of the 1970s the national aircraft industries of the two largest South American countries were in a state of healthy expansion, each developing aircraft of its own design for both civil and military applications. In Argentina, military aviation products are the responsibility of the Fábrica Militar de Aviones, a part of the Area de Material Córdoba Division of the Fuerza Aérea Argentina. Founded in 1927, it subsequently underwent various name changes (including, in 1943, that of Instituto Aerotécnico, whose initials are still borne by current designs) before reverting to its original title in 1968. Chief designer and engineer for many years has been Vicecomodoro H. E. Ruiz, and the latest of his products is the I.A.58 counter-insurgency aircraft, design of which was initiated in August 1966. The original configuration, for a twin-tailboom aircraft with a central crew nacelle, was later shelved in favour of a more conventional layout. Preliminary flight trials were conducted with an unpowered, full-size aerodynamic prototype with dummy engine nacelles and non-retractable landing gear; this was flown for the first time on 26 December 1967, and in the following February detail design of the first powered prototype was started. This aircraft, designated AX-01, flew for the first time on 20 August 1969, and was powered by 904 e.h.p. TPE 331 turboprop engines. The AX-02 second prototype, which first flew on 6 September 1970, has 1,022 c.h.p. Turboméca Astazou XVIG turboprops; this powerplant was later selected for the production version, and by early 1974 work had begun on an initial quantity of one hundred Pucarás, in which are included five pre-production aircraft for service trials and thirty production aircraft to meet an initial order from the Fuerza Aérea Argentina. A crew of two is carried, on tandem-mounted ejection seats, and the Pucará has a fixed armament of two 20 mm. Hispano cannon and four 7·62 mm. FN machine-guns mounted in the underside of the nose. There is a single stores point under the fuselage and one beneath each outer wing panel, each capable of carrying a variety of gun pods, bombs and rockets or a 66 gallon (300 litre) auxiliary fuel tank. A design for a training aircraft, based on the Pucará and powered by two side-mounted Astafan turbofan engines, was disclosed in 1973.

13 Aérospatiale N 262 and Frégate

Derived from the 22-seat Max Holste M.H.250 Super Broussard feederliner design of 1957, the twin-turboprop Aérospatiale (former Nord-Aviation) N 262 passenger transport (see *Airliners since 1946*) has had most of its modest success in the civil market. The original Series A and B, with Turboméca Bastan VIC turboprop engines, were later followed by the Frégate, with more powerful 1,145 e.h.p. Bastan VIIs giving improved performance at 'hot and high' airfields. The Aéronavale ordered fifteen Series As in June 1967 for use as aircrew trainers, and six were built for the Armée de l'Air, which in the spring of 1969 placed a second contract, for eighteen Frégates for use on training and liaison duties. Prior to delivery of the Aéronavale machines, the civil Nord 262 F-WNMP was leased to the French Navy (as F-YCKY) to get its training programme started. Systems and installations developed for this version enable it to carry out, in addition to transport duties, basic aircrew training for navigators and radio operators of patrol aircraft (e.g. the Breguet Atlantic); aerial photography; radar calibration duties; marker dropping; target towing for ships' anti-aircraft weapons training; and spotting duties during gunnery and missile practice. Except in the aircrew training role, a flight crew of 3 and a flight technician are normally carried.

The Armée de l'Air aircraft have a normal flight crew of 3; they accommodate up to 29 troops in the transport role, 18 when used as a paratroop trainer, or 4 stretchers and seats for 16 other persons in an aeromedical configuration.

14 Scottish Aviation Jetstream

First announced in January 1966 as the Handley Page H.P.137, the Jetstream was originally conceived as a twin-turboprop light transport aircraft, with accommodation ranging between 8-seat executive and 20-seat commuter layouts. It appeared to have a bright future, for Riley Jetstream Corporation of America had then ordered twenty, increasing this figure to eighty-five at the end of 1966; C.S.E. Aviation later ordered a hundred; and the U.S. Air Force ordered eleven with AiResearch TPE 331 engines as C-10As for the V.I.P. transport role. The initial design powerplant, the Turboméca Astazou XIV, was not available for the first flight by G-ATXH on 18 August 1967, which was therefore made with a temporary installation of Astazou XIIs; the first flight with Astazou XIVs followed on 29 November 1967. In all, Handley Page built this prototype, one structural test aircraft, four pre-production and thirty-six Mk 1 production Jetstreams before going into liquidation, and many of these are still in civilian service in the U.K., Europe and North America. Test flying of the Mk 3M, the prototype military version for the U.S.A.F., had begun in November 1968, but Handley Page's collapse brought cancellation of the C-10A order while many of these aircraft were still in the assembly stage. Scottish Aviation, which had been building Jetstream wings under sub-contract, eventually acquired the entire Jetstream project, and is currently executing an order for twenty-six Jetstream T. Mk 1s for the Royal Air Force, to replace the Varsity as a flying classroom for pilots of multi-engined aircraft. The first of these (XX475) was flown for the first time on 13 April 1973. Deliveries, initially to the Central Flying School and No. 5 Flying Training School, began later that year, and the first course of students to train on these aircraft began flying in Jetstreams in July 1974. Four trainees can be carried, in addition to the flight crew of two. The R.A.F. Jetstreams have the manufacturer's designation Series 200 (Model 201), and are an outgrowth of the original Handley Page proposal for a Mk 2 aircraft. After completion of the R.A.F. order, in 1975, Scottish Aviation plans to proceed with a civil Series 200 version. This will be generally similar to the Model 201 but with Astazou XVI C2 engines, different avionics, no 'eyebrow' windows above the flight deck, and cabin seating for up to 18 passengers.

15 Lockheed F-104 Starfighter

Lockheed's Starfighter is one of those instances, that occur every so often, of an aeroplane that disappoints in the role for which it was first intended, only to blossom out later and excel at a quite different task. Thus it was that only two hundred and seventy-seven Starfighters of the first four marks were built, as short-range day interceptors and fighter-trainers; whereas the multi-mission F-104G, for tactical support and reconnaissance missions, became the subject of the biggest international co-operative manufacturing programme in Europe since World War 2.

Lockheed built two XF-104s

with 10,000 lb. (4,409 kg.) st Wright XJ65-W-6 engines, the first of which was flown on 7 February 1954, followed by an evaluation batch of fifteen YF-104s. Initial production models, for Air Defense Command and Tactical Air Command of the U.S.A.F., were the single-seat F-104A (one hundred and fifty-three built, first flight 17 February 1956); 2-seat F-104B (twenty-six built, first flight 7 February 1957); single-seat F-104C (seventy-seven built); and 2-seat F-104D (twenty-one built). Thirty-six F-104As were sold to Jordan, twelve to Pakistan and twenty-five F-104Bs to China. Twenty F-104 DJs for the J.A.S.D.F. were assembled by Mitsubishi from Lockheed-built components. Thirty F-104Fs, basically similar to the D, were built for the Federal German Luftwaffe.

Major changes introduced with the single-seat F-104G were a much-strengthened airframe, upward (instead of downward) ejection seat, and enlarged vertical tail surfaces. The F-104G was built, by German, Dutch and Belgian consortia, for the Luftwaffe (six hundred and four), the Dutch Koninklijke Luchtmacht (ninety-five) and the Force Aérienne Belge (ninety-nine); and for the Aeronautica Militare Italiano (one hundred and twenty-four) and the Royal Netherlands Air Force (twenty-five) by Fiat and Aermacchi in Italy. Lockheed-built F-104Gs were supplied to Germany (ninety-six), Belgium (one) and Italy (one). Lockheed also built one hundred and eighty-one 2-seat TF-104Gs.

Variants of the F-104G include the CF-104 (two hundred built by Canadair for the R.C.A.F., which also received thirty-eight Lockheed-built CF-104D trainers); and the F-104J for the Japan Air Self-Defence Force. The J.A.S.D.F. had two hundred and ten of these, most of which were built under licence by Mitsubishi. Canadair production also included U.S.-financed F-104Gs for Denmark (twenty-five), Greece (thirty-six), Norway (sixteen), Spain (twenty-five) and Turkey (thirty-eight). Standard fixed armament of the F-104G, which flew for the first time on 5 October 1960, is a 20 mm. Vulcan multi-barrel cannon, augmented by two or four Sidewinders for interception missions. In the attack role, two Bullpup missiles, two rocket pods, three 1,000 lb. (or two 1,000 lb. and one 2,000 lb.) bombs, three land mines or one tactical nuclear weapon are among the many possible external loads. Production of all these versions is complete, but in Italy in 1974 production continued, by Aeritalia (Fiat), of two hundred and five F-104Ss for the A.M.I., a strengthened model with a 17,900 lb. (8,120 kg.) st J79-GE-19 engine and nine external armament points; the first F-104S was flown on 30 December 1968. Weapons include bombs and rockets, and Sidewinder or Sparrow air-to-air missiles. Turkey has ordered eighteen of this version.

16 Northrop T-38 Talon

Possessing the distinction of being the first training aeroplane to be designed from the outset for flight at supersonic speeds, the Talon entered service in March 1961 with Air Training Command of the U.S.A.F. The Talon, whose first YT-38 prototype (58-1191) was flown on 10 April 1959 with non-afterburning YJ85-GE-1 engines, set out as a supersonic replacement for the veteran Lockheed T-33A, but is capable of covering all stages of advanced and tactical training previously conducted with the Cessna T-37, the T-33 and the F-86F Sabre or F-100F Super Sabre. Final familiarisation is given on the 2-seat version of the type which the trainee will fly operationally. The Talon is also employed by N.A.S.A., which acquired twenty-four to give spaceflight readiness training to America's astronauts; and five U.S.A.F. aircraft were procured by the U.S. Navy. The Federal German Luftwaffe ordered forty-six which, delivered in 1967, fly in the U.S.A. in U.S.A.F. markings and are used to train German student pilots. The thousandth T-38A was delivered in January 1969; one thousand one hundred and eighty-nine were built, the last being delivered in January 1972. Although it clearly has much in common with the Northrop F-5 strike fighter which was evolved from it, the Talon has lower-powered engines and lacks the F-5's wing leading-edge flaps. It has the outstanding initial climb rate of 30,800 ft. (9,388 m.) per minute, which secured for it several climb-to-height records in 1961.

17 & 18 Northrop F-5

Four years of indecision and apparent indifference followed the maiden flight, on 30 July 1959, of Northrop's N-156F Freedom Fighter, a compact, nimble and versatile design aimed at the smaller air forces of the world which needed up-to-date but none-too-expensive equipment. Northrop built, as a private venture, three prototypes of the N-156C (as it was originally known), in parallel with the N-156T 2-seat trainer version which became the T-38A Talon. The third prototype, representing an improved model and designated N-156F, flew for the first time in May 1963, by which time the U.S. Defense Department had selected the type, in single-seat F-5A and 2-seat F-5B forms, for delivery under its Military Assistance Program to several N.A.T.O. and S.E.A.T.O. air forces. The first production F-5A was flown in October 1963, and the first foreign delivery, a squadron of thirteen, was made to the Imperial Iranian Air Force in February 1965. Iran eventually received one hundred and four F-5As, thirteen RF-5As and twenty-two F-5Bs, of which some have in recent years been returned to the U.S. for allocation to South Vietnam; some have also reportedly been transferred to Pakistan. Subsequent recipients have included the air forces of Nationalist China, Ethiopia, Greece, Libya, Morocco, Norway, South Korea, the Philippines, Thailand and Turkey. Orders from Northrop production had totalled six hundred and twenty-one F-5As (including reconnaissance RF-5As) and one hundred and thirty-four F-5Bs by the beginning of 1974. In addition, CASA of Spain assembled thirty-six SF-5As and thirty-four SF-5Bs for the Ejército del Aire; Canadair built one hundred and fifteen of an improved model (eighty-nine CF-5As and twenty-six CF-5Ds) for the Canadian Armed Forces, and seventy-five NF-5As and thirty NF-5Bs for the Royal Netherlands Air Force. The F-5A and F-5B have broadly similar performances, the F-5B dispensing with the single-seater's two 20 mm. Colt-Browning M-39 guns and carrying a second crew member. Both models have provision for up to 6,200 lb. (2,812 kg.) of stores on five external stations, and a Sidewinder air-to-air missile at each wingtip.

In response to the Defense Department's IFA (International Fighter Aircraft) programme for an F-5 successor for M.A.P. countries, Northrop re-engined an F-5B with two 5,000 lb. (2,268 kg.) st YJ85-GE-21 turbojets and modified the airframe for improved performance, fuel load and operational versatility. This prototype, designated YF-5B-21, flew for the first time on 28 March 1969, and in November 1970 this version (now redesignated F-5E) was selected in preference to variously-modified developments of the Lockheed F-104, McDonnell Douglas F-4 and Vought F-8 to fulfil the M.A.P. requirement.

Major airframe differences in the F-5E include a wider fuselage; increased-area wings, extended forward in a wing/body airflow strake at the roots and having full-span leading-edge flaps; and an improved fire control system. Airfield performance is improved (there is a runway arrester hook and provision for J.A.T.O.), and so is manoeuvrability. The F-5E is intended primarily for the air superiority role, with two nose-mounted M-39 20 mm. cannon and a Sidewinder at each wingtip. It can, however, carry up to 7,000 lb. (3,175 kg.) of ordnance, on one under-fuselage and four under-wing stations, in the ground attack role.

First flight of a production F-5E was made on 11 August 1972, and by the autumn of 1973 about twenty were in service at Williams Air Force Base to train pilots of the recipient air forces. These include Jordan, South Korea, Taiwan, Thailand and South Vietnam under M.A.P.; paying customers include Brazil (thirty-six), Chile, Iran (one hundred and forty-one), Malaysia, and Saudi Arabia (thirty). Brazil and Saudi Arabia have, in addition, ordered six and twenty F-5Bs respectively. First recipient was South Vietnam, which received its first four F-5Es in March 1974 and also has on order twenty-eight examples of the 2-seat F-5F currently being developed. Deliveries of F-5Es totalled forty-eight in 1973; a further one hundred and fifty-eight were due to be delivered in 1974, and two hundred and fifty in 1975.

19 Lockheed T-33

Belgium, Brazil, Canada, Chile, Nationalist China, Colombia, Cuba, Denmark, Ecuador, Ethiopia, France, Germany, Greece, Iran, Italy, Japan, Korea, Mexico, the Netherlands, Nicaragua, Norway, Pakistan, Peru, the Philippines, Portugal, Saudi Arabia, Spain, Thailand, Turkey, Uruguay, the United States, Venezuela and Yugoslavia – such is the impressive list of more than thirty nations with whose air arms the T-33 has flown since it first made its appearance in 1948. It was on 22 March of that year that aircraft 48–356, modified and then designated TF-80C, made its maiden flight as a 2-seat conversion trainer variant of America's first service jet fighter, the F-80 Shooting Star. Between 1949 and 1959, more than five thousand eight hundred T-33 series aircraft (one thousand and fifty-eight of them for M.A.P. distribution) were built by Lockheed, who also supplied parts for a further two hundred and ten assembled by Kawasaki in Japan. Canadair built six hundred and fifty-six more as the CL-30 (R.C.A.F. name Silver Star), most of these having 5,100 lb. (2,313 kg.) st Rolls-Royce Nene engines. American-built T-33As at first had two 0·50 in. M-3 machine-guns for armament training, but these were omitted from later production aircraft. The version used by the U.S. Navy was designated TV-2 originally, T-33B later; the Navy/Marine Corps orders for this version totalled six hundred and ninety-nine. The RT-33A (eighty-five built) was a single-seater equipped with cameras for aerial reconnaissance; the Netherlands, Pakistan, Thailand and Turkey were among the recipients of this version. The T-33As supplied to the Hellenic Air Force were ex-R.C.A.F. Silver Stars. It says much for the qualities of this aeroplane that in 1974 it was still in service with many of the nations listed above; indeed, a new customer was about to be added: Bolivia, for whose air force NWI of Canada was refurbishing thirteen ex-Canadian Armed Forces' T-33As.

20 Aérospatiale (Fouga) Magister

The C.M. 170 Magister was not only one of the world's first production jet trainers, but has also been among its most successful, equipping the two main French air arms in substantial numbers and serving with those of many other countries besides. Three prototypes (the first flown on 23 July 1952) and ten pre-production machines were followed by preliminary French orders for ninety-five Magisters for the Armée de l'Air and thirty-two CM.175 Zéphyrs (the 'hooked' version for carrier use) for the Aéronavale. Subsequent orders brought the total number of Magisters for the Armée de l'Air to four hundred, and the type has been employed for many years past as the mount of that force's Patrouille de France aerobatic team. Fouga, the original design and manufacturing company, later became a part of the Potez group and subsequently of Sud-Aviation, now Aérospatiale. During production of the Magister these companies supplied sixty-two to the West German Luftwaffe, for whom Heinkel and Messerschmitt (Flugzeug-Union-Süd) completed a further one hundred and eighty-eight; Finland's Ilmavoimat received twenty from France before having a further sixty-two built under licence in the country by Valmet; and thirty-six Bedek-built machines by Israel Aircraft Industries were included in the fifty-two Magisters completed for the Israeli Air Force. In addition to these, French-built Magisters were delivered to Belgium and Holland (forty-eight), the Österreichische Luftstreitkräfte (eighteen), Royal Khmer Aviation of Cambodia (four), the Force Aérienne Libanaise (four) and the Forces Aériennes Congolaises (six). Magisters for French service included the Super Magister, one hundred and thirty of which are included in the total above. Except for its power plant of two 1,058 lb. (480 kg.) st Marboré VI engines the Super Magister, which first flew on 28 August 1962, is basically similar to the original model. With its arrival in service, some of France's earlier Magisters were transferred to the Algerian and Moroccan Air Forces, and six others have been ordered by the Irish Air Corps. Seven Super Magisters were supplied to the Fôrça Aérea Brasileira. The Magister has provision for two 7·5 mm. or 7·62 mm. nose guns, and four 55 lb. (25 kg.) rockets, two 110 lb. (50 kg.) bombs, two Matra launchers each for eighteen 37 mm. or seven 68 mm. rockets, or two AS.11 anti-tank missiles underwing.

21 **Hispano HA-200 Saeta (Arrow) and HA-220 Super Saeta**

Professor Willy Messerschmitt led the Hispano-Aviación team which produced the HA-200, drawing extensively on both the design and the actual components of his HA-100 Triana piston-engined trainer; the entire outer wing and rear fuselage units are the same on both types. Two prototypes were completed, the first of these flying on 12 August 1955; these were joined in the test programme, after a prolonged gestation period, by ten pre-production aircraft, five of which were completed to HA-200B standard. The first of these was flown on 21 July 1960. The Saeta has tandem seating in a fully pressurised cabin, with twin Marboré turbojets mounted side by side below the cockpits and exhausting at the wing trailing-edge roots. Deliveries to the Escuela de Reacción (Jet School) of the Ejército del Aire, by whom it is known as the E-14, comprised thirty HA-200As (first flight 11 October 1962) and fifty-five improved HA-200Ds (first flight April 1965). Hispano built five additional examples of the HA-200B, with Marboré IIA engines and one 20 mm. Hispano-Suiza cannon; all ten were supplied to Egypt, where this model was built under licence at Helwan as Al-Kahira (the Cairo). The Egyptian programme called for the manufacture of ninety aircraft, but it is not known if all were completed before the closure of the Helwan Air Works in 1969. A marked improvement in performance is exhibited by the HA-200E, one hundred of which were built for the Ejército del Aire with 1,058 lb. (480 kg.) st Marboré VI engines and improved avionics. Modifications increase the maximum take-off weight to 7,937 lb. (3,600 kg.), at which the HA-200E has a maximum speed of 429 m.p.h. (690 km./hr.) at 22,975 ft. (7,000 m.) and a service ceiling of 42,650 ft. (13,000 m.). The initial rate of climb at an all-up weight of 5,840 lb. (2,650 kg.) is 3,050 ft. (930 m.) per minute, compared with the 2,755 ft. (840 m.) per minute of the HA-200D. Armament consists of two 7·7 mm. Breda machine-guns and two underwing Matra 38 carriers for a variety of rocket launchers, bombs, guns or reconnaissance equipment.

In December 1967 the Spanish government ordered twenty-five examples of an HA-220 Super Saeta ground attack version which has the military designation C-10-C. The prototype HA-220 flew for the first time on 25 April 1970. This has essentially the same airframe and powerplant as the HA-200E, but is converted to single-seat configuration, has increased fuel capacity in self-sealing tanks, armour protection for vital areas, and modified internal equipment. Possible weapon loads include a variety of gun and rocket armament and bombs on six attachment points, two under the fuselage and two beneath each wing.

22 Rockwell International T-2 Buckeye

The Buckeye was evolved in the late 1950s as a low-cost, multi-stage trainer for the United States Navy, with whom it has been in service since 1959. Its design relied on systems already proven in other North American products, employing a substantially similar wing to the original FJ-1 Fury and a cockpit controls system akin to that used by the piston-engined T-28C trainer. Though a straightforward and unspectacular aeroplane, the Buckeye is nevertheless capable of training naval pilots right through from the *ab initio* flight stage to the full range of manoeuvres required on board the U.S. Navy's aircraft carriers. The T-2A has two underwing attachment points from which 0·50 in. gun pods, 100 lb. practice bombs or pods of 2·75 in. rockets can be suspended for weapons training. The first two prototypes were originally designated XT2J-1, and the first of these (144217) was flown on 31 January 1958. Two hundred and seventeen examples of the single-engined T2J-1 (redesignated T-2A in 1962) were built up to early

1961; on 30 August 1962, one of these was flown with an experimental installation of two smaller 3,000 lb. (1,361 kg.) st Pratt & Whitney J60-P-6 engines in place of the single J34. After a second such conversion, ten similar aircraft, designated T-2B, were completed for evaluation by the U.S. Navy; the first of these was delivered to Training Squadron 7 in November 1965, and follow-on contracts for T-2Bs increased the total ordered to ninety-seven. The first production T-2B was flown on 21 May 1965, and deliveries to the U.S.N. began in 1966. Following its first flight on 17 April 1968, Rockwell began production of the T-2C, a second twin-engined model, powered by 2,950 lb. (1,339 kg.) st J85-GE-4 engines but otherwise generally similar to the T-2B. One hundred and eighty-three T-2Cs had been ordered by early 1974, and funding for a further twenty-four was requested in the FY 1974 budget. Forty T-2Cs have been ordered by the Greek Air Force. Delivery took place in 1973 of twelve T-2Ds to the Venezuelan Air Force; this model is basically similar to the T-2C but with the carrier landing equipment deleted and some changes in avionics. The T-2A was phased out of U.S. Navy service in early 1973, having been replaced entirely by the B and C models.

23 HAL HJT-16 Kiran (Ray of Light)

The Kiran, which bears a superficial resemblance to (and uses the same powerplant as) the British Jet Provost, was the first jet aircraft to be designed and built wholly by a team of Indian engineers.

Design began in April 1961, to meet an Indian Air Force requirement for a basic and intermediate jet trainer to replace the Vampire, and was undertaken at the Bangalore Division of Hindustan Aeronautics Ltd. under the leadership of Dr V. M. Ghatage. Major assembly of the first prototype began in November 1963, and this aircraft (U327) was flown for the first time on 4 September 1964. A second prototype flew in August 1965. Hindustan Aeronautics, then already building the Bristol Siddeley Orpheus engine under licence, selected the same company's Viper 11 engine, of 2,500 lb. (1,135 kg.) thrust, as the Kiran's powerplant. The side-by-side 2-seat cockpit is fully pressurised and air-conditioned, and is fitted with Martin-Baker Mk H4 HA lightweight ejection seats and dual controls. Provision is made for the carriage of two 50 gallon (227 litre) underwing auxiliary fuel tanks, which can be replaced if required for armament training or counter-insurgency duties by a pair of 7·62 mm. twin-gun pods, eight 3 in. T10 rockets, twelve 68 mm. rockets or four 25 lb. practice bombs. Delivery of twenty-four pre-production aircraft began in March 1968; about a hundred and fifty production Kiran Mk Is are expected to be built, of which some thirty-six had been delivered by the end of 1973, including seven to the Indian Navy.

24 WSK-Mielec TS-11 Iskra (Spark)

Two years of study, of a variety of configurations, went into the TS-11 before the design was finalised late in 1958; work was under the supervision of Ing Tadeusz Soltyk, who was responsible for the earlier TS-8 Bies piston-engined trainer. Protracted attempts were then made, first with Bristol Siddeley and then with Turboméca, to acquire a suitable foreign engine, but when these failed the Polish aircraft industry decided to evolve one of its own. With this the first of four Okecie-built prototypes was flown on 5 February 1960. Polish pilots are reported to be enthusiastic about its handling qualities, and when in 1962 the Iskra came a very close second to the Czech Delfin in the competition to find a basic trainer for the Warsaw Pact countries, the Polish government turned down the winning aircraft in favour of its own design. About ten pre-production TS-11s, the first of which was flown in November 1962, had been delivered to the Polskie Lotnictwo Wojskowe by mid-1963, some of which, like the prototypes, were powered by a 1,764 lb. (800 kg.) st HO-10 turbojet engine. Supplies of production aeroplanes began later that year; by the end of 1965 the Iskra had virtually replaced the TS-8 in training squadrons, although a few hours *ab initio* training is still given on piston-engined types before passing on to jets. The Iskra, still in production in 1974, with several hundred having been built, has a similar general layout to the American Temco TT-1 of the late 1950s, but is a more advanced aircraft. It has a fully pressurised cabin, two ejection seats, and is convertible to the armament training role. The latter version, designated Iskra-100, is fitted with a 23 mm. cannon in the starboard side of the nose and has four underwing racks for 50 kg. bombs, rockets or other stores.

25 Canadair CL-41 and CT-114 Tutor

Lack of support from the Canadian government in 1958 might have marked the early demise of the Tutor jet basic trainer; indeed, the project did lie dormant for more than a year before Canadair decided to pursue it as a private venture. The result was that, by coming rather late into a field already highly competitive, the Tutor was able to embody much experience gained by others of its kind, causing the R.C.A.F. to change its mind to the extent of an order for a hundred and ninety aircraft. It is an all-Canadian product; the engine was designed by the Montreal branch of Pratt & Whitney, and its economy of operation and first-class thrust-to-weight ratio play no small part in the Tutor's efficiency. The first of two CL-41 prototypes (CF-LTW-X) flew on 13 January 1960, powered by a 2,400 lb. (1,089 kg.) st JT12A-5 turbojet engine, and production aircraft began to be delivered in October 1963. 'All-through' jet training with the Tutor started early in 1965, by which time over sixty CL-41A aircraft were in service under the CT-114 designation. Deliveries were completed during 1966. The Tutor is somewhat heavy by basic trainer standards, but this, coupled with a particularly good operational radius, made it well suited for adaptation to ground attack duties. Accordingly, the fifteenth CL-41A airframe was modified to serve as prototype for such a version, the CL-41G, and flew for the first time in June 1964. The CL-41G has a 2,950 lb. (1,338 kg.) st J85-J4 engine, soft-field landing gear and zero-height ejection seats. It carries no fixed armament, but its six external stores points can support gun or rocket pods, Sidewinder missiles, bombs, napalm canisters or auxiliary fuel tanks up to a total load of 3,500 lb. (1,583 kg.). In March 1966, twenty CL-41Gs were ordered by the Royal Malaysian Air Force; delivery of these began in 1967 and was completed early in 1969. They are known in service by the name Tebuan (Wasp). A low-level reconnaissance proposal, designated CL-41K, was not built, and no production was undertaken of the CL-41R, an experimental systems trainer version with N.A.S.A.R.R. avionics in an extended 'needle' nose. This aircraft, which flew for the first time on 13 July 1962, was converted from CF-LTX-X, the second prototype.

26 Aermacchi M.B.326

Some of the best aircraft of World War 2, from the point of view of pilot handling, were the Macchi fighters; thus it is no surprise that one of the world's leading jet basic trainers, a category in which good flying characteristics are all-important, should come from the same stable. The M.B.326 prototype made its first flight on 10 December 1957. An order for one hundred for the Aeronautica Militare Italiano was fulfilled early in 1966 (they began to enter service in January 1962) and basically similar training models were produced for Alitalia (four M.B.326D with airline-type avionics) and the Royal Australian Air Force. The first thirty M.B.326Hs for the R.A.A.F. (of eighty-seven ordered) were assembled under licence in Australia by Commonwealth Aircraft Corporation from Italian-built components; the remaining fifty-seven, plus ten for the Royal Australian Navy, were built entirely in Australia. The M.B.326C (which was not built) was a projected version for the training of F-104G pilots, modified to mount a Starfighter-type nose radome and N.A.S.A.R.R. equipment.

The Viper 11-powered M.B.326 was also built as a dual-role trainer/light-attack aircraft for the Armée de l'Air Tunisienne (eight M.B.326B), Ghana Air Force (seven M.B.326F) and South African Air Force (M.B.326M Impala, assembled initially from Italian-built components but later built almost entirely under licence in South Africa by Atlas Aircraft Corporation). Impala production, about one hundred and fifty, was completed in 1974. The M.B.326B and F models have twin 7·7 mm. machine-guns (with a camera gun in the nose) and six underwing pylons on which the loads may include various combinations of 0·50 in. machine-gun pods, Matra 122 packs of 68 mm. air-to-air rockets, 5 in. HVAR rockets, a reconnaissance pod with four 70 mm. Vinten cameras, 260 lb. (118 kg.) bombs or underwing drop-tanks. Armament of the M.B.326M, which is somewhat heavier, can include two 12·7 mm. gun packs, two SUU-11 General Electric 7·62 mm. Minigun packs and two 6 × 80 mm. SURA rocket packs; two Miniguns with two Matra 361 packs of thirty-six 37 mm. FFAR rockets and two 500 lb. (227 kg.) bombs; two Miniguns and two napalm tanks; or two Nord AS.11 air-to-surface missiles. A more powerful dual-role version, with a 3,410 lb. (1,547 kg.) st Viper 20 Mk 540 engine, first made its appearance in the form of the M.B.326G, which flew for the first time in the spring of 1967. The production version is designated M.B.326GB. The Aviación Naval Argentina has ordered eight, seventeen have been ordered by the Zaïre Republic and twenty by Zambia. Major customer up to early 1974 was the Fôrça Aérea Brasileira, for whom one hundred and twelve M.B.326GCs are being assembled under licence in Brazil by EMBRAER as the AT-26 Xavante.

In 1970 Aermacchi announced details of the M.B.326K (referred to originally as the M.B.336B), which is essentially a single-seat trainer or ground attack aircraft based on the airframe of the M.B.326GB. It is, however, powered by a 4,000 lb. (1,814 kg.) st Viper Mk 632-43 engine, and has a built-in armament of two 30 mm. DEFA cannon, leaving the six underwing points free for the carriage of bombs, rocket armament or auxiliary fuel tanks. The prototype M.B.326K flew for the first time on 22 August 1970; Aeritalia reportedly has supplied four to Atlas in South Africa as a prelude to major production in that country. A 2-seat version of the K, designated M.B.326L, was announced in 1973.

27 **Aero L-29 Delfin (Dolphin)**
The first design studies for this sturdy and competent jet trainer were made in 1955, by a team under the leadership of K. Tomas and Z. Rublic. The prototype XL-29, which had a Bristol Siddeley Viper jet engine, was test-flown on 5 April 1959 by Rudolf Duchon of the Československé Závody Letecké, a Czechoslovak state aircraft company. The nationally-designed M-701 jet engine was introduced as the definitive powerplant on the second prototype (which flew in July 1960) and pre-production aircraft. With tandem seating for pupil and instructor, the Delfin covers both the primary and intermediate stages of flying

training; it can also be employed as an armaments trainer or for light attack duties, there being underwing points which can take bombs, gun or rocket pods or auxiliary fuel tanks. In the early 1960s the Delfin was chosen, in preference to Russia's Yak-32 and Poland's TS-11, as the standard initial trainer for the air forces of the Warsaw Pact nations. The first production L-29 was completed in April 1963; approximately three thousand three hundred had been built by the beginning of 1974, more than two thousand of these having been supplied to the Soviet Union (where the first Delfin squadron was formed at Ivano-Frankovsk in May 1963) and to the air forces of Bulgaria, East Germany, Hungary and Romania. Those in Soviet service have the N.A.T.O. code name 'Maya'. Czechoslovakia had about four hundred. About a dozen were supplied late in 1964 to the Angkatan Udara Republik Indonesia; other recipients include the air forces of Egypt, Iraq, Nigeria, Syria and Uganda. Variants of the basic L-29 include the L-29R counter-insurgency version, and the L-29A Delfin Akrobat, a single-seat aerobatic version for use in military and civil sporting displays. Neither of these is believed to have been produced in great quantity, but they remain available as variants of the standard production aircraft.

28 Aero L-39 Albatros

At the time of the Soviet invasion in 1968 the Czechoslovak aircraft industry had under active development several interesting new types of military aircraft. Among these was the L-39 basic and advanced jet trainer, the first prototype of which (OK-32) was flown for the first time on 4 November 1968 by Rudolf Duchon. This was actually the second L-39 airframe to be completed, the first having been one of two built for structural test. One cause of the apparently slow development of the aircraft was the delays with the Soviet-designed turbofan engine, considerable modification of which by Czech engineers was reported necessary. By late 1970, when five prototypes were known to have flown, these had been or were being modified to have larger and slightly longer intake trunks to improve the efficiency of the Czechoslovak-built AI-25-T version. Ten pre-production L-39s were completed in 1971, and production aircraft began to enter service with the Czech Air Force in 1973. The L-39, which, like the L-29 before it, has a tandem 2-seat layout, is designed to perform at speeds of up to Mach 0·83, as compared with its predecessor's limit of Mach 0·75. It was designed by a team under the leadership of Dipl Ing Jan Vlcek, and is intended as a replacement for the Delfin, military production of which had already exceeded three thousand between 1963 and 1973 for the air forces of the Warsaw Pact nations, and was expected to be phased out by about 1975. The Ceskoslovenské Letectvo requirement for the type has been reported as being for three hundred, with a similar quantity to be produced for the U.S.S.R. and other customers. One L-39 prototype has been test-flown with under-wing and under-fuselage weapon loads, and an L-39Z light strike version is thought to have been ordered by the Iraqi Air Force.

29 **Cessna T-37 and A-37**
As the U.S. Air Force's first aircraft designed from the outset as a primary and intermediate jet trainer, the Cessna T-37 marked a departure from the practice of years by adopting a side-by-side seating arrangement. The first of three XT-37s flew on 12 October 1954, and these were followed by eleven T-37A evaluation aircraft. This original production model was powered by 920 lb. (417 kg.) st Continental J69-T-9 engines (licence version of the French Marboré II), and a further five hundred and twenty-three were completed. With 1,025 lb. (465 kg.) st J69-T-25 (Marboré VI) engines and other refinements the aeroplane became known as the T-37B, and the T-37As also were eventually converted to T-37B standard. From 1960, all U.S.A.F. trainee pilots commenced their tuition on T-37s, but in 1965 it was decided that a few hours on T-41 piston-engined trainers before transition to jets would prove more economical. After this, T-37 pilots would normally graduate to the Northrop T-38A. The T-37B trainer (four hundred and forty-seven built) was also sold to foreign air forces under the Military Assistance Program, as was the T-37C (two hundred and fifty-two built), an armed version with provision for two 250 lb. (113 kg.) bombs, two gun or rocket pods or four Sidewinder missiles underwing. Recipients of the T-37 included the West German Luftwaffe (forty-seven T-37B), the Fôrça Aérea Brasileira (sixty-five T-37C), the Fôrça Aérea Portuguesa (thirty T-37C), the Fuerza Aérea del Perú (fifteen T-37B), and the Cambodian (T-37C), Chilean (T-37B/C), Colombian (ten T-37C), Royal Hellenic (twenty T-37B), Pakistan (twelve T-37B), Royal Thai (eight T-37B) and Turkish (T-37B) air forces.

Cessna also produced two prototypes designated YAT-37D, a higher-powered armed attack version for service in Vietnam. The first of these was flown on 22 October 1963, and in 1966 the U.S.A.F. ordered thirty-nine T-37Bs to be converted to similar standard under the designation A-37A. This version, which became operational in October 1967, has eight underwing stores points for two machine-gun pods, two 2·75 in. rockets, and four practice bombs; or, in place of the gun pods, two 250 lb. bombs or four Sidewinder missiles. The A-37B, built from the outset for the same role, has 2,850 lb. (1,293 kg.) st J85-GE-17A engines, provision for in-flight refuelling, and a much wider variety of underwing ordnance, up to a maximum load of

5,680 lb. (2,576 kg.). The first A-37B was flown in September 1967, and deliveries began in May 1968. Orders for the A-37B totalled four hundred and sixteen by mid-1973, including twenty-four for Peru and others for the U.S.A.F. and the air forces of Chile (sixteen), Guatemala and South Vietnam.

30 Soko Galeb (Gull) and Jastreb (Hawk)

After the end of World War 2 the Yugoslav state-owned aircraft industry concentrated chiefly on light civil aircraft, piston-engined trainers and research machines, drawing its main military equipment from the Soviet Union or the U.S.A. In the late 1950s, a trio of small twinjet aircraft made their appearance under the general designation of Type 451. None achieved production status, but it seems likely that their designer, Major Dragojub Beslin, was involved in development of the Galeb, Yugoslavia's first production jet aircraft. Two prototypes of the Galeb were completed, flight testing beginning in May 1961, and the Soko works at Mostar, near Sarajevo, subsequently built it in quantity for the Jugoslovensko Ratno Vazduhoplovstvo, with whom it entered service during 1965. Basic production model was the G2-A primary and intermediate trainer, powered by a 2,500 lb. (1,134 kg.) st Viper 11 Mk 22–6 turbojet engine and having a gross weight ('clean') and maximum speed of 8,439 lb. (3,828 kg.) and 505 m.p.h. (812 km./hr.) respectively. Approximately sixty were reported in service in late 1972. For armament training or light attack duties the Galeb can be fitted with two 0·50 in. machine-guns in the nose and underwing carriers for two 110 lb. (50 kg.) or 220 lb. (100 kg.) bombs and either four 57 mm. or two 12·7 cm. rockets. In November 1969 Soko began building a Galeb-3 prototype, with a 3,395 lb. (1,540 kg.) st Viper Mk 532 engine, gross weight of 10,600 lb. (4,803 kg.), and a maximum speed of 497 m.p.h. (800 km./hr.) with an external weapons capability similar to that of the J-1 Jastreb. The Galeb-3 flew for the first time on 19 August 1970, but did not go into production.

The Jastreb, which entered production for the Yugoslav Air Force in 1968, is a single-seat and more powerful development of the G2-A. It has provision for two 1,000 lb. (454 kg.) JATO (jet-assisted take-off) rockets to be attached beneath the fuselage to augment the Viper 531 powerplant during take-off and flight, three nose-mounted 12·7 mm. machine-guns (135 r.p.g.) and eight underwing attachments for weapons or other stores. About thirty Jastrebs were in Yugoslav service at the end of 1972. Four Jastrebs and two Galebs were supplied to the Zambian Air Force.

31 & 32 BAC Jet Provost and Strikemaster

Anyone fortunate enough to have seen the Jet Provost in the hands of a skilled demonstrator can have no doubts that the 'JP' is one of the most agile aeroplanes now flying; and its almost viceless handling qualities have for years made it an ideal *ab initio* trainer. As an early C.F.S. report observed, the pupil achieves 'a more dexterous and better mental approach to the art of modern flying. His repertoire of aerobatic manoeuvres ... is generally much more extensive, and flown with more accuracy and spirit.' A development batch of ten Mk 1 aircraft was built, the first of these (XD674) flying for the first time on 26 June 1954. The tenth machine (XD694) became the T. Mk 2 production prototype, flying for the first time on 1 September 1955 and preceding the T. Mks 3 and 4 production models for the R.A.F. The latter version was powered by a 2,500 lb. (1,134 kg.) st Viper 202 engine. The Mks 3 and 4 were delivered to the R.A.F. from August 1959 and November 1961 respectively, the T. Mk 3 having flown for the first time on 22 June 1958. Two hundred and one Mk 3's and one hundred and eighty-five Mk 4's were built for the R.A.F. Its tractability has also made the 'JP' an ideal close support and 'police' aircraft, and the colour plate shows one of the Royal Ceylon Air Force's twelve T.51s, armed version of the T.3; this version was also supplied to Kuwait (six) and the Sudan (four). The armed T.4, known as the T.52, was purchased by the Fuerzas Aéreas Venezolanas (fifteen), the Iraqi Air Force (twenty), Sudan (eight) and South Yemen (four). Twin 0·303 in. Browning machine-guns are mounted in the air intake walls, and the underwing stations allow for a diversity of external loads including bombs, rockets, flares and rocket projectiles. Full dual controls exist in all versions, and the T.51 and T.52 can perform both armament training or fully operational combat duties equally well.

The BAC 145, which flew for the first time on 28 February 1967, has the same engine as the T.4 but a completely new front fuselage (incorporating a pressurised cockpit with an even better view), a shorter rear fuselage, more fuel space in the wings and a better performance. The final two T. Mk 4s (XS230 and 231) were converted to serve as prototypes. The BAC 145 entered production for the R.A.F. as the Jet Provost T. Mk 5, to replace earlier models; a hundred and ten were ordered, and delivery of these (commencing XW287) took place between September 1969 and October 1972. Five of a slightly heavier armed version were delivered to the Sudan Air Force as the Mk 55.

Current member of the family is the BAC 167 Strikemaster light ground-attack aircraft, which utilises the basic BAC 145 airframe with a more powerful Viper Mk 535 engine and can carry up to 3,000 lb. (1,360 kg.) of assorted stores – gun or rocket pods, bombs, napalm tanks, reconnaissance pods or drop-tanks – on eight underwing attachments. A prototype was flown on 26 October

1967, and by spring 1974 one hundred and twenty-nine Strikemasters had been ordered by Saudi Arabia (twenty-five Mk 80 and ten Mk 80A), South Yemen (four Mk 81), Oman (twelve Mk 82 and eight Mk 82A), Kuwait (twelve Mk 83), Singapore Air Defence Command (sixteen Mk 84), Kenya (six Mk 87), New Zealand (sixteen Mk 88) and Ecuador (sixteen Mk 89); the remaining four were a repeat order for the Sultan of Oman's Air Force.

33 Saab 105

The Saab 105 is a multi-purpose aeroplane which is equally at home as a 2-seat military trainer, 4/5-seat liaison aircraft, reconnaissance or light attack aeroplane. It is in the first and last of these categories that it is primarily employed by the Swedish Flygvapnet. The first private-venture design studies for a jet successor to the Safir were undertaken in 1959, but Saab had decided to use twin engines to achieve a high safety factor and completion was delayed by the lack of a sufficiently small engine with adequate power. Eventually the French Turboméca company evolved the little Aubisque turbofan, and when the first of two prototype Saab 105s flew on 29 June 1963 its engines were also making their first flight. The first of a hundred and fifty SK 60 production aircraft was flown on 27 August 1965 and deliveries to F5, the Swedish Air Force Flight Training School, began in the spring of 1966; these aircraft were integrated into the training system from mid-1966, trainee pilots graduating to the SK 60A after about 30 hours on the piston-engined Safir. Other versions in Swedish service are designated SK 60B and SK 60C. The SK 60A and B are both used primarily in the training role, but have, respectively, limited or complete provision for rapid adaptation as ground-attack aircraft. In the latter role the six underwing stores points can carry two 30 mm. cannon pods, two 250 kg. or six 125 kg. bombs, two 300 kg. RB05 radio-guided air-to-surface missiles, twelve 13·5 cm. rockets or other loads up to a total of 1,543 lb. (700 kg.). The SK 60C was first flown on 18 January 1967; this is a version of the SK 60B with a permanently-installed panoramic-type reconnaissance camera installed in a modified nose.

In 1970–71 production was undertaken of forty Saab 105Ö for the Österreichische Luftstreitkräfte, delivery of which began in the spring of 1970. These are based on the Saab 105XT export model, first flown on 29 April 1967, which has more powerful 2,850 lb. (1,293 kg.) st General Electric J85-GE-17B turbojets giving an enhanced performance at higher operating weights, including up to 4,410 lb. (2,000 kg.) of external ordnance. In 1970 Saab offered Switzerland the Saab 105XH, with a built-in 30 mm. Aden cannon, permanent wingtip fuel tanks, modified avionics and further increase in weapon-carrying capability, but no production orders were received. Latest version, which flew for the first time on 26 May 1972, is the Saab 105G, a further development of the version produced for Austria.

34 de Havilland Vampire Trainer

The D.H.100 Vampire was the second British jet-propelled aeroplane to go into quantity production, the fighter prototype first flying on 20 September 1943. It was subsequently built on a wide scale as a fighter and fighter-bomber for the R.A.F. and Commonwealth air forces, and still survived in small numbers in 1973 in the inventories of such air arms as those of the Dominican Republic, New Zealand, Rhodesia, South Africa, Switzerland and Venezuela. The D.H.115 Vampire Trainer, distinguishable by its broader canopy, covering side-by-side seats, and by its dorsal fin extensions, was evolved by de Havilland as a private venture, flying for the first time on 15 November 1950. Nine hundred and thirteen Trainers were built for a score of air forces, including those built under licence in Australia and India. Many of these were still active in 1973 as advanced trainers with the air arms of Australia, Austria, Burma, Chile, India, the Irish Republic, Lebanon, Portugal, Rhodesia, South Africa, Switzerland and Venezuela. The R.A.F. trainer version, first flown (WW548) on 1 December 1951, was the T. Mk 11 (its F.A.A. counterpart being the Sea Vampire T. Mk 22). Full dual controls and two ejection seats are installed, together with a fixed armament of two 20 mm. cannon, enabling the D.H.115 to be used as a gunnery trainer or, suitably modified, as a light attack aircraft. Eight hundred and four Vampire Trainers were built in Britain, including seventy-three Sea Vampire T. Mk 22s and fifty-five T. Mk 55s for the Indian Air Force. Fifty of the latter were assembled in India by Hindustan Aircraft Ltd. Six refurbished T. Mk 22s were supplied to Chile in 1973. In Australia, de Havilland Aircraft Pty. Ltd. built thirty-six T. Mk 33s for the R.A.A.F. and five T. Mk 34As for the Royal Australian Navy, followed by sixty-eight T. Mk 35s (with extra fuel capacity) for the R.A.A.F. The T. Mk 33s were later brought up to T. Mk 35 standard and redesignated T. Mk 35A.

35 North American F-86D/K/L Sabre

Such was the success of the Sabre (first flown on 1 October 1947) as a day fighter and fighter-bomber that it was logical for its further development to include a version evolved for all-weather interception. Development of such a version, which became the F-86D, was begun early in 1949, and a YF-86D prototype (one of two built) flew for the first time on 22 December 1949. The F-86D was unusual in remaining a single-seat aeroplane, when all contemporary practice dictated a second crew member to cope with the additional radar and electronics. Growing pains associated with this equipment kept the Sabre from full effectiveness in its new role until mid-1953, although it had entered U.S.A.F. service over two years earlier. The F-86D, as the first all-weather version was known, had virtually a new fuselage, embodying a 'chin' intake under a bulbous nose radome, and a retractable ventral pack of twenty-four 2·75 in. rockets instead of a gun armament. From 1958 the U.S. dispersed many of its F-86Ds to other countries, recipients including the air forces of Nationalist China, Denmark (thirty-eight), Greece (fifty), Japan (one hundred and six), South Korea, the Philippines (eighteen), Turkey (fifty) and Yugoslavia (one hundred and thirty). Two thousand five hundred and four F-86Ds were built – the largest production of any single Sabre model – and of these nine hundred and eighty-one were converted to extended-span F-86Ls, with more advanced avionics, to serve as a part of America's SAGE (Semi-Automatic Ground Environment) defence system. Some F-86Ls were also delivered to the Royal Thai Air Force. An export version of the D model, evolved for N.A.T.O. air forces, was the F-86K, which had four 20 mm. M24A-1 cannon and two Sidewinders to replace the fuselage rockets. Production of the F-86K totalled three hundred and forty-one, built between 1954 and 1958.

Of these, one hundred and twenty were completed by North American; the remainder were assembled by Fiat in Italy, the final forty-five being completed with the extended-span wings, with modified leading-edges, of the L model. American-built F-86Ks, including the two YF-86K prototypes, were supplied to the Norwegian (sixty) and Dutch air forces (fifty-nine). Italian-built examples were delivered to the Italian Air Force (sixty-three), and to France (sixty), Germany (eighty-eight), the Netherlands (six) and Norway (four). The Dutch aircraft were later transferred to Turkey.

36 North American F-100 Super Sabre

The Super Sabre, whose YF-100A prototype (the first of two) flew for the first time on 25 May 1953 after four years design work, deserves its niche in aviation history as the first fully supersonic warplane to go into quantity production. It began life under the company designation Sabre 45, the figures indicating the degree of wing sweepback; but subsequent development was such as to render it a completely new design. First production model was the F-100A day fighter, two hundred and three of which were built with 9,700 lb. (4,400 kg.) st J57-P-7 or -39 engines, four 20 mm. M-39E cannon and six stores attachment points. The F-100A, first flown on 29 October 1953, began to arrive in U.S.A.F. service in September 1954; eighty, brought up to F-100D standard, were supplied to the Chinese Nationalist Air Force. The F-100C, first flown on 17 January 1955, was a fighter-bomber version with a 7,500 lb. (3,402 kg.) external load on eight strong-points and able to refuel in flight. Production totalled four hundred and seventy-six, of which two hundred and sixty were later released to the Türk Hava Kuvvetleri. A number of design refinements, including a taller fin, appeared in the F-100D (first flight 24 January 1956), which entered production in that year. In addition to the standard quartet of 20 mm. cannon, the F-100D can carry four Sidewinders and, for attack missions, two Bullpup missiles and/or a wide variety of conventional weapons up to a maximum of 7,500 lb. (3,402 kg.). The F-100D was the major production version, one thousand two hundred and seventy-four being built, and was used extensively by the U.S.A.F. in Vietnam in 1966–71. Others were supplied under M.A.P. terms to the French and Danish air forces. Final version of the Super Sabre, which brought total production to two thousand two hundred and ninety-two before completion in October 1959, was the 2-seat F-100F, which flew for the first time on 7 March 1957 following the flight of a TF-100C prototype on 6 August 1956. Three hundred and thirty-nine F-100Fs were built. With two 20 mm. cannon and a 6,000 lb. weapons load, this model could perform either tactical attack roles or combat training duties. The Danish and Turkish forces, as well as the U.S.A.F., received quantities of the F-100F.

37 & 38 Hawker Hunter

The Hunter is one of those aeroplanes that deserve the term 'thoroughbred' applied to its design and has been an outstanding success for many years both as an export item and as a piece of military equipment. The first of three Hawker P.1067 prototypes (WB 188) flew on 20 July 1951, and the first production Mk 1 (WT555) on 16 May 1953. Early production Hunters were specifically transonic day fighters; the Hawker-built Mks 1 (one hundred and thirty-nine built) and 4 (three hundred and sixty-five built) each had Avon engines, while the forty-five Mk 2s and one hundred and five Mk 5s built by Armstrong Whitworth were Sapphire-powered. Of these the Mk 4 was produced for the R.A.F., for Denmark (thirty Mk 51), Peru (sixteen Mk 52) and Sweden (one hundred and twenty Mk 50). A more powerful Avon, a 'dog-tooth' wing leading-edge and a 'flying' tail marked the Hunter F.6, the major single-seat version, which could carry a heavier range of external stores than its predecessors. The prototype Mk 6 (XF833) was flown on 22 January 1954; two hundred and sixty-four were built by Hawker, and one hundred and nineteen by Armstrong Whitworth. The F(GA). Mk 9 was a ground-attack conversion for the R.A.F. in the Middle and Far East; the FR. Mk

10 a three-camera reconnaissance conversion of the F.6; and the GA. Mk 11 an attack trainer for the Royal Navy, converted from the F.4 with no cannon but an extensive range of stores. Altogether Hunter production, including two-seaters and four hundred and forty-five Mks ;. and 6 built in Holland and Belgium, amounted to one thousand nine hundred and seventy-seven; hundreds were still in service in 1974. Equivalents of the F. Mk 6 were supplied to the air forces of India (one hundred and sixty Mk 56), Iraq (thirty-five Mk 59), Jordan (two Mk 60), the Lebanon (thirteen Mk 59) and Switzerland (one hundred Mk 58). India and Switzerland later re-ordered Mk 56A and sixty Mk 58A respectively. Versions of the F(GA). Mk 9 and FR Mk 10 have included four Mk 57s for Kuwait, and others for the Abu Dhabi Defence Force (Mk 76 and Mk 76A), Chilean Air Force (Mks 71/71A), Jordanian Air Force (Mks 73/73A/73B), Qatar (four Mk 78), Rhodesian Air Force (twelve) and Singapore Air Defence Command (sixteen Mks 74/74A). Many of those Hunters exported have been diversions from R.A.F. orders or refurbished ex-R.A.F. aircraft. Hunters first entered service with the R.A.F. (No. 43 Squadron) in July 1954, and enjoyed a length of service equalled by few aircraft of any nationality. No. 111 Squadron's 'Black Arrows' and No. 92's 'Blue Diamonds' provided the R.A.F's aerobatic team for five years in succession. The Hunter is extremely versatile in the attack role, carrying a considerable variety of stores on four underwing stations; typical loads include sixteen 60 lb. (27 kg.) rockets, two 500 or 1,000 lb. (227 or 454 kg.) bombs, napalm tanks or auxiliary fuel tanks. Some Dutch and Swedish F.4s were adapted to carry a pair of Sidewinder air-to-air missiles.

A 2-seat version of the Hunter day fighter was a logical development, and a requirement issued in 1954 confirmed the need for such an operational conversion trainer for the R.A.F. Hawker produced the first prototype two-seater (XJ615), or T. Mk 7 as it was to become known, in quick time, its first flight taking place on 8 July 1955. It was basically an adaptation of the single-seat F. Mk 4, with a new and longer front fuselage including a dual-control side-by-side cockpit under a new 'hooded' canopy, and only a single Aden cannon on the starboard underside. The R.A.F. was supplied from mid-1958 onwards with fifty T. Mk 7s, including five converted from F.4s; a further twenty went to the Koninklijke Luchtmacht; the Fleet Air Arm counterpart was the 'hooked' T. Mk 8, of which twenty-eight were produced, including eighteen converted from F.4s; Denmark's Flyvevåbnet had two Mk 53s, and the Fuerza Aérea del Perú one Mk 62. Similar modifications were made to the more powerful Hunter F.6, except that both the Adens were retained, yielding the Mk 66 (twenty-two for India), Mk 66B (one for Jordan), Mk 66C (Lebanon), Mk 66D (India), Mk 67 (two for Kuwait), Mk 69 (Iraq/Lebanon), Mk 70 (Jordan), Mk 72 (three for Chile), Mk 75 (four for Singapore), Mk 77 (Abu Dhabi) and Mk 79 (two for Qatar). Overall production of 2-seat Hunters, which included many conversions, amounted to one hundred and one aircraft.

39 **Saab 32 Lansen (Lance)**
A handsome and workmanlike aeroplane, the initial A 32A version of the Lansen was delivered to attack squadrons of Sweden's Flygvapnet in December 1955; it began to be replaced by the AJ 37 Viggen in 1971, but is expected to remain in service, in diminishing numbers, until 1975. The Lansen originated with Saab's project R119 for an all-weather attack aircraft powered by two de Havilland Ghost turbojet engines, superseded in October 1948 by Project P1150, a cheaper and less complex design based on the Swedish STAL Dovern jet engine. Due to development delays with this engine, Saab adopted instead the Rolls-Royce Avon Series 100, and modified a Safir trainer (designated Saab 202) to flight-test the wings of the new aircraft. Four Saab 32 prototypes were built, and the first of these (serial number 32001), with a 7,500 lb. (3,402 kg.) st Avon RA.7 engine, was flown for the first time on 3 November 1952. The Lansen was built in three basic versions, for attack (A 32A), night and all-weather fighter (J 32B), and day and night photographic reconnaissance missions (S 32C). The last Lansen, a J 32B, was completed on 2 May 1960, when four hundred and fifty had been built over a period of some seven years. The A 32A, which was the first to go into service, carries a fixed armament of four 20 mm. Swedish Hispano cannon; attack loads, on the four underwing stations, comprise four RB04 anti-shipping missiles, twelve 100 kg. or four 250 kg. bombs (or two 500 kg. on the inner stations only), or up to twenty-four air-to-air rockets; powerplant is an afterburning Rolls-Royce Avon RA.7R turbojet. Four attack wings – F6, F7, F14 and F17, comprising twelve squadrons – were eventually equipped with the A 32A. The J 32B, with an 11,023/15,190 lb. (5,000/6,890 kg.) st RM6B (Series 200) Avon and a Swedish-designed afterburner, was first flown on 7 January 1957 and had an effective combination of four 30 mm. Aden M55 cannon and four underwing rocket pods or RB324 (Sidewinder) missiles. It entered service in July 1958, serving with F12 and F1 (three squadrons each) and one squadron of F21, but has now been phased out of first-line service. The unarmed, RM5-engined S 32C, built in parallel with the J 32B and first flown on 26 March 1957, continued in service with F11 in 1974. It can be fitted with a variety of different camera installations according to the nature of the mission. The Lansen was the

first Swedish aeroplane successfully to exceed sonic speed (in a dive – its level performance is slightly below Mach 1); all versions seat a crew of two.

40 Fuji T-1

The Fuji T-1's cockpit layout is similar to that of an earlier J.A.S.D.F. jet trainer, the Lockheed T-33A, and doubtless much else that was learned from the American type went into the planning of the first jet aircraft to be designed and built in quantity in Japan after the end of World War 2. Originating as the T1F1, the trainer was intended to utilise a Japanese-designed turbojet engine, but as an interim step two T1F2 prototypes were completed with Bristol Siddeley Orpheus engines and the maiden flight of the type was made by one of these aircraft on 19 January 1958. The first flight of a T1F1 with a 2,645 lb. (1,200 kg.) st Ishikawajima J3 engine took place on 17 May 1960. The Fuji Jukogyo subsequently built forty T-1As (T1F2s) with 4,000 lb. (1,814 kg.) st Orpheus 80506 engines and twenty Japanese-engined T-1Bs (T1F1s) for the J.A.S.D.F. Delivery of all sixty aircraft was completed by mid-1963. One of the prototypes was converted to T-1C (T1F3) configuration by installing a 3,085 lb. (1,400 kg.) st J3-IHI-7 engine, with which it first flew in April 1965; this version was demonstrated – unsuccessfully – in 1965 to the R.A.A.F., who chose Italy's M.B. 326 instead, and a proposal to re-engine the J.A.S.D.F's T-1Bs to a similar standard was cancelled. Like most jet trainers, the T-1A can, if needed, double as a close support aircraft, mounting a 0·50 in. machine-gun and carrying bombs, rockets or Sidewinder missiles up to a maximum load of 1,500 lb. (680 kg.) on underwing pylons.

41 Mikoyan/Gurevich MiG-17 ('Fresco')

It was in January 1950 that Artem Mikoyan recorded the first flight of this derivative of his famous MiG-15 fighter, but the MiG-17 did not enter Soviet Air Force service until 1953. Subsequently, however, it was built in Russia, China, Czechoslovakia and Poland on a scale which may well have exceeded that of the MiG-15, and served with the forces of more than a score of countries for a remarkably long period. Many of these air arms have since re-equipped with supersonic MiG-21 fighters, but MiG-17s could still be found in 1974 in the inventories of nearly a score of air forces, particularly in Asia, the Middle East and Africa. Fresco-A was the initial production MiG-17, a day fighter with a 5,952 lb. (2,700 kg.) st non-afterburning VK-1A engine and an armament of two 23 mm. and one 37 mm. cannon. The MiG-17P Fresco-B was its limited all-weather interceptor counterpart, distinguished by its 'lipped' air intake and small centrebody radar. Most Fresco operators received either the MiG-17F (Fresco-C) day fighter or

MiG-17PF (Fresco-D) limited all-weather fighter. The MiG-17F was the major production version, being built also under licence in Poland (as the LiM-5P), Czechoslovakia (as the S-104) and China (as the Shenyang F-4). A multi-purpose day fighter, it had a fixed armament of three 23 mm. NR-23 cannon; provision for bombs, unguided rockets or drop-tanks under the wings; was powered by the VK-1F afterburning version of the Klimov engine; and was fitted with larger airbrakes. The MiG-17PF also appeared in a MiG-17PFU version (Fresco-E), with its cannon armament deleted in favour of a quartet of Alkali air-to-air missiles. Polish designers evolved a 'battlefield' version of the MiG-17F, designated LiM-5M, with deeper, longer-chord inboard wing panels housing extra fuel and twin-wheel main landing gear units with low-pressure tyres. A limited number of this model, produced by converting existing LiM-5Ps, served with the Polish Air Force in the late 1960s, but preference was given to a less complicated conversion, the LiM-6, to which standard many earlier Polish MiG-17s were eventually modified. A photographic version was designated LiM-6R.

42 Dassault Super Mystère B-2

Development of the Mystère IVA led Dassault to produce, in 1953, a Mystère IVB variant with a Rolls-Royce RA.7R afterburning turbojet engine and a 'lipped' intake similar to that of the North American Sabre. Continued evolution of this version led to the prototype Super Mystère, first flown on 2 March 1955, which embodied a new wing, of greater sweep and thinner aerofoil section and having a 'dog-tooth' leading-edge, an enlarged vertical tail, a flat-oval air intake and improved cockpit view for the pilot. On its fourth test flight this aircraft exceeded the speed of sound in level flight, and when the Super Mystère was placed in production in 1956 it was the first European-designed service aircraft with a Mach 1 performance. First flight of a production Super Mystère was made on 26 February 1957. Primarily a single-seat day interceptor and tactical strike fighter, the Super Mystère carries a twin-cannon armament (30 mm. DEFA), has a fuselage pack of fifty-five Type 22 air-to-air rockets, and two underwing stations can each support six HVAR rockets or a Matra nineteen-rocket pod. These weapons can be replaced by napalm canisters or 500 kg. bombs. The Armée de l'Air aircraft were also equipped to carry a Sidewinder air-to-air missile beneath each wing. The five pre-production test aircraft had the same powerplant (Atar 101G) as the one hundred and eighty production Super Mystères, twenty-four of which were supplied to the Israeli Air Force, with whom the type still served in 1974. The first production aircraft began to enter service with the Armée de l'Air in 1957, and delivery was completed in 1959. Two Escadres of the French Air Force were still operating about thirty Super Mystères in 1974, but their replacement by the Mirage F1 was then imminent.

The Super Mystère B-4 was one aircraft fitted experimentally as a flying test-bed for the SNECMA Atar 9 turbojet (13,250 lb.= 6,010 kg. st with afterburning) and flown for the first time on 9 February 1958.

43 Dassault Étendard IV

The name Étendard (flag) was originally applied to a land-based tactical support fighter, the Étendard II, which had two Turboméca Gabizo turbojet engines and first flew on 23 July 1956. Neither this nor the Étendard VI (one Orpheus engine, first flight 15 March 1957) went further than the prototype stage, though the latter was entered for the N.A.T.O. light fighter competition won eventually by the Fiat G91. The true precursor of the production interceptor/strike/reconnaissance model was the private-venture Étendard IV, flown for the first time on 21 May 1958. The Étendard IV has been in service with France's Aéronavale since it began to replace the French Navy's piston-engined Corsairs in April 1962, completing the substitution in 1964. Six pre-production aircraft (five IV-Ms and one IV-P) were completed. The ninety aircraft subsequently built comprised twenty-one Étendard IV-P (= photographique) tactical reconnaissance models, which can also act as 'buddy' tankers; nineteen Étendard IV-M (=marine) strike fighters with similar tanker equipment; and a further fifty IV-Ms without that facility. Production ended in 1965. Early in 1965 all Étendards were temporarily grounded after a series of accidents in which fourteen aircraft were lost; they returned to operational status with altitude and range restrictions, and in 1974 still equipped three Flottilles (11F, 16F and 17F) in the carriers *Foch* and *Clémenceau* and one training unit (Flottille 15F). The Étendard IV-M has one or two 30 mm. DEFA cannon mounted in the lower fuselage, and four underwing attachment points for up to 3,000 lb. (1,360 kg.) of ordnance, including two AS.30 missiles (the antenna for which is housed in the triangular strake beneath the aeroplane's nose) and two Sidewinders, rocket pods, two 225 or 400 kg. bombs, or auxiliary fuel tanks. The ventral cannon bay of the IV-M is occupied in the IV-P by two vertical cameras, with another three cameras in the nose. All Étendards are single-seaters.

Following its rejection of the Jaguar M naval version, the Aéronavale has chosen instead a developed version of the Étendard, a prototype of which flew on 28 October 1974. Known as the Super Étendard, this will have an 11,023 lb. (5,000 kg.) st Atar 8K-50 engine, a more up-to-date radar in a much-enlarged nose, and improved avionics and wing high-lift devices. It is intended to replace the Étendard IV in 1976–77; one hundred Super Étendards were ordered in August 1973.

44 Mikoyan MiG-19 ('Farmer')

It was in 1950 that the Mikoyan design collective began work on what was to become the Soviet Union's first supersonic fighter to achieve squadron status. The design, based upon the use of two small-diameter Mikulin AM-5 turbojets mounted side by side in the rear of the fuselage, received official approval on 30 July 1951 and the first prototype, designated I-350, was flown in September 1953. A small initial production batch, with 4,850/6,700 lb. (2,200/3,040 kg.) st AM-5F engines, entered service in early 1955, first being seen by Western observers at the Aviation Day display that summer, in which forty-eight of them took part. This model suffered from elevator troubles, and with its somewhat unbalanced armament of one 37 mm. and two 23 mm. cannon was probably not produced in very great numbers; at any rate a new model, the MiG-19S (Farmer-A) day fighter, began to enter service in 1956. This retained the AM-5 powerplant, but was armed with three of the faster-firing 30 mm. NR-30 cannon (one in each wing root and one beneath the nose on the starboard side), had a one-piece 'slab' tailplane, wing spoilers and a third, ventral airbrake to supplement those on either side of the fuselage aft of the wings. Some two years later this in turn was succeeded by a new model, the MiG-19SF (Farmer-C), which was to become the standard day fighter version. The change of designation indicated the introduction of more powerful RD-9B engines in place of the AM-5s. Both the MiG-19S and MiG-19SF were provided with two stores attachment points beneath each wing, the outer pair being occupied more usually by fuel tanks and the inboard pair (located aft of the main landing gear) by unguided air-to-air rockets. Contemporary with the MiG-19SF was a limited all-weather version, the MiG-19PF (Farmer-B). This had a nose section some 1 ft. 9½ in. (0.55 m.) longer than the day fighter versions, with a 'lipped' air intake and a small, hemispherical centrebody radome mounted on the air intake splitter plate. The undernose gun was deleted, and two leading-edge weapon-launching shoes, usually carrying pods of unguided rockets, replaced the inboard pair of aft-mounted pylons. A more fully-developed all-weather version was the MiG-19PM (Farmer-D), in which the two wing-root guns were also deleted and the number of inboard leading-edge pylons increased to four, each capable of carrying an 'Alkali' air-to-air missile. Some aircraft of this version have been seen with modified cockpit canopies offering forward and sideways vision only.

Production of MiG-19 aircraft

was on a large scale; although believed to have ended in the U.S.S.R. in 1959, it also included licence production in Czechoslovakia (as the S-105) and (as the Shenyang F-6) in the Chinese People's Republic. Chinese-built F-6s equivalent to the MiG-19SF have been supplied to the air forces of Pakistan (about 90), these having provision for carrying Sidewinder air-to-air missiles and including a number employed in the ground-attack role or for fighter-reconnaissance duties; and Tanzania (about thirty). China has also produced the MiG-19PF. In addition to the countries mentioned, MiG-19s of various models were also supplied to the air forces of Bulgaria, Cuba, Egypt, the German Democratic Republic, Indonesia, Iraq, Romania and Yugoslavia, several of which were still operating the type in 1974. The Chinese F-9 attack fighter, of which about three hundred were reported to be in service by early 1974, is almost certainly a developed version of the F-6 with more modern avionics and other improvements.

45 Sukhoi Su-7BM ('Fitter-A') and Su-17 ('Fitter-B')

The primary function of Sukhoi's Su-7B Fitter-A is that of close support and ground-attack fighter. It differs from the Su-9 and Su-11 'Fishpot' (*q.v.*) in employing a sharply-swept wing (62 degrees) of very thin section, which probably renders it more manoeuvrable than its delta-winged stablemate, particularly at the slower over-the-target speeds needed for an aircraft of this type. At the same time, the extreme thinness and sharp sweep are factors which limit the size and weight of potential underwing stores. These usually comprise two 750 kg. or 500 kg. bombs, or two pods of unguided rockets. Fixed armament consists of two 30 mm. wing-root guns. Twin fuel tanks (or two 500 kg. bombs) can be carried side by side beneath the centre fuselage; other aircraft have been seen with fuel tanks on the underwing pylons and a rocket pod on one of the under-fuselage stations. The single-seat Su-7BM is currently used by the Soviet Air Force, with whom it has been in service since about 1960, and was the first production warplane to come from the Sukhoi design bureau after it was re-established in 1952. Its first public appearance, in prototype form, was in the Aviation Day display at Tushino in 1956, when it was powered by a 14,330/19,840 lb. (6,500/9,000 kg.) st afterburning turbojet engine. Production aircraft have also been supplied to the air forces of Cuba, Czechoslovakia, Egypt, East Germany, Hungary, India, Poland, Syria and North Vietnam. The initial production Su-7B lacked the now-standard twin dorsal strakes and large tail-chute fairing at the base of the rudder which characterise the Su-7BM. A tandem 2-seat training version, the Su-7UTI, is code-named 'Moujik'. Reports during the 'Yom Kippur war' in the Middle East in 1973, of a side-by-side 2-seat operational version with the designation Su-20, were not substantiated by photographic evidence, and it seems more likely that these aircraft were export versions of the single-seat swing-wing Su-17 Fitter-B.

At Domodedovo Airport in July 1967 the Soviet authorities demonstrated what the official commentator described as the country's first variable-geometry aircraft. Now understood to have been designated Su-7E, this prototype was essentially a standard Su-7BM airframe, except that the wing panels outboard of the main landing gear had leading-edge slats and could pivot to give a wing span of about 41 ft. (12·50 m.) in the fully-forward position. Three closely-spaced fences are fitted to the fixed portion of each wing, the outer fence on each side extending over the full chord and having stores attachments built into the underside. Other characteristics are generally similar to the Su-7BM, with the probable exception of a longer range and shorter take-off and landing runs. In its Su-17 production form, Fitter-B is in Soviet Air Force service in some quantity, and has also been supplied to Poland. Production aircraft have a large dorsal spine fairing and other detail differences; the wing-root guns and inboard wing leading-edge pylons are retained. The Su-20 is a version of the Su-17 with additional inboard hardpoints, giving it an improved ground attack capability.

46 Hawker Siddeley Gnat

Forerunner of the 2-seat Gnat Trainer, described separately, the single-seat fighter was the version originally conceived by W. E. W. Petter, Folland's chief designer, and first flew on 18 July 1955 after experimental flying with the even smaller Folland Midge, which was first flown on 11 August 1954. Great Britain had never officially declared a requirement for a light-weight fighter like the Gnat, although the idea never lacked for advocates. The Ministry of Supply ordered six for evaluation and the Yugoslav government two, although neither placed any further order. The first production aircraft was flown on 26 May 1956. However, the Finnish government bought a dozen for the Ilmavoimat in 1958, two of them having blunted noses containing three reconnaissance cameras. This squadron was still in service in Finland in 1970. The Gnat's biggest success was in India, to whom twenty-five complete aircraft and components for another fifteen were supplied from Britain in the summer of 1959. After this, the fighter was built under licence in India by Hindustan Aeronautics Ltd. from 1962, production being stepped up in 1965 after the Gnat's excellent showing in the clash over Kashmir. The total number of Gnats built for the Indian Air Force, presumably including the fifteen assembled from British-built components, was two hundred and fifteen. The first was completed in 1962, and production ended in

1973. The Gnat, in both its forms, is a supremely agile transonic aeroplane. The single-seater has a good take-off and landing performance, tight turn, and fast climb and roll rates; a 30 mm. Aden cannon is mounted in the outer lip of each air intake, and there are underwing stores points on which two drop-tanks, two 500 lb. (227 kg.) bombs or twelve 3 in. rockets can be carried for close support missions.

A Mk II version, reportedly named Ajeet (Unconquerable), is under development by HAL and was expected to fly in prototype form in the summer of 1975. Essentially, this will retain the existing airframe, but will have an uprated Orpheus engine and a 'wet' wing, permitting an increase in external weapons load.

47 Hawker Siddeley Gnat Trainer

The 2-seat advanced trainer version of the Gnat is, if anything, even more a masterpiece of packaging than the fighter. In a basically similar airframe only some 15 per cent larger, a second cockpit, additional fuel tankage, TACAN and ILS equipment have all been added as against the removal of the fighter's twin gun packs. The first Gnat Trainer was flown on 31 August 1959, after an order the previous year for fourteen pre-production aircraft for the R.A.F. These and a further ninety-one production Gnat Trainers, ordered between July 1960 and March 1962, began to join Flying Training Command squadrons from January 1962. They assumed the role formerly filled by the Vampire T.11, of providing the second stage of R.A.F. training after the Jet Provost and were still in service in 1974. One of the favourite display aircraft of recent years, notably with the R.A.F's 'Yellow Jacks' and later with the 'Red Arrows' aerobatic team, the 2-seat Gnat has a truly outstanding manoeuvrability, including a maximum roll rate of 200 degrees per second. Nominally capable of Mach 1·15 in a shallow dive, it was, with the uprating of the Orpheus 101 to 4,400 lb. (1,996 kg.) st, enabled to reach Mach 1·26. The cabin is fully pressurised, and the Folland-designed ejection seats provide escape at all heights down to ground level. The excellent landing qualities of the aircraft, particularly at low speeds, are enhanced in the trainer version by the greater wing area.

48 Gloster Javelin

The world's first twin-engined delta-winged aeroplane to go into production, the Javelin was also the first British production aircraft designed specifically for the all-weather fighter role. Its entry into service was not achieved without some development difficulties, and although four hundred and twenty-eight production aircraft were built for the Royal Air Force these did not have the versatility that the range of nine Mark numbers might imply. Not until the advent of the Mk 7, able to carry four Firestreak infra-red homing missiles in addition to the standard fixed armament of four wing-mounted 30 mm. Aden cannon, could the Javelin be regarded as a viable all-weather fighter in the modern understanding of the term. Gloster built four G.A.5 flying prototypes (WD804, WD808, WT 827 and WT830) conforming to Specification F.4/48, and the first of these was flown on 26 November 1951 with two 7,000 lb. (3,175 kg.) st Armstrong Siddeley Sapphire non-afterburning engines. Modifications to the wings, ailerons, radome and cockpit canopy were tested on the prototypes, and the first production order was placed in mid-1953. First production Javelin to fly, on 22 July 1954 was XA544, the first of forty F(AW). Mk 1 (XA544-572, XA618-628) powered by 8,300 lb. (3,765 kg.) st Sapphire 102/103 engines. Twenty-five of these were used for various kinds of development work, including XA552 which was refitted with de Havilland Gyron Junior and XA565 with Rolls-Royce Avon RA.24R afterburning engines. A prototype with U.S. APQ-43 instead of British A117 radar (XD158) was flown on 31 October 1955, preceding thirty F(AW). Mk 2 (XA768-781, XA799-814) with similar radar and a hydraulically-actuated 'all flying' tailplane instead of the Mk 1's electrically-actuated elevators. The T. Mk 3 was a dual-control, tandem 2-seat operational trainer version, with a lengthened no-radar nose; WT841, the prototype (built by Air Service Training and first flown 20 August 1956), was followed by an initial Gloster-built production batch of twenty (XH390-397, XH432-438, XH443-447), plus two replacement aircraft (XK577, XM336), delivered to No. 228 O.C.U. Application of the all-flying tail to the Mk 1 airframe resulted in the F(AW). Mk 4, production of which totalled fifty aircraft (XA629-640, XA644, XA763-767 by Gloster; XA720-737, XA749-762 by Armstrong Whitworth); the first Mk 4 was flown on 19 October 1955. The F(AW). Mk 5 was basically the Mk 4 with a redesigned wing housing increased fuel: sixty-four were built (XA641-643, XA645-661 by Gloster; XA662-667, XA688-719, XH687-692 by Armstrong Whitworth); XA641 flew for the first time on 24 August 1956. The thirty-three F(AW). Mk 6s (XA815-836, XH693-703, first flight 15 January 1957) were essentially similar to the Mk 2 but incorporating the Mk 5 wing. Major production version, of which one hundred and forty-two were built, was the F(AW). Mk 7. This was a developed version of the Mk 5, with Firestreak missiles, two Aden cannon instead of four, and more powerful 200-series Sapphire engines; the prototype (XA560), which flew for the first time on 30 September 1955, was converted from a Mk 1, and production aircraft (XH704-725, XH746-784, XH900-912, XH955-965 by Gloster; XH785-795, XH833-849, XH871-899 by Armstrong Whitworth) began to enter service in 1958. The final Javelin production model was the F(AW). Mk 8, basically similar to the Mk 7 except that engine afterburners and different radar were fitted. The first of forty-seven Mk 8s (XH966–993, XJ113–130, XJ165) was flown for the first time on 9 May 1958 and the last was completed in mid-1966. The designation F(AW). Mk 9 applied to forty-six Mk 7 aircraft fitted with afterburning. The Mks 8 and 9 had provision for in-flight refuelling equipment. A batch of eighteen 'thin wing' Javelins was also ordered, but these were later cancelled.

The Javelin first entered service, with No. 46 Squadron, in February 1956, and subsequently served also with Nos. 5, 11, 23, 25, 29, 33, 41, 60, 72, 85, 87, 89 and 151 Squadrons. In addition to U.K. service it was employed during its career in Germany, the Middle East, Far East and (following Rhodesia's U.D.I.) Zambia, the last Javelin being withdrawn from service in 1967.

49 Hawker Siddeley Sea Vixen

A standard all-weather fighter from 1959 until the early seventies, operated by the Fleet Air Arm from both aircraft carrier bases and shore stations, the Sea Vixen began life as the de Havilland D.H.110 back in the late 1940s, the first of two prototypes (WG236), powered by two 6,500 lb. (2,948 kg.) st Avon RA.3 engines, making its maiden flight on 26 September 1951. It was a contemporary of the Javelin and, although conceived initially for naval use, was first evaluated as a competitor to the Gloster type for R.A.F. orders. Arising out of Naval specifications N.40/46 and N.14/49, the higher-powered second prototype (WG 240), which first flew on 25 July 1952, was modified for evaluation by the Royal Navy as a carrier-based all-weather fighter. Structural changes included an increase in outer-wing chord to give a 'dog-tooth' leading-edge, the fitting of an 'all-flying' tailplane and a reduction in the ventral fin area. It was ordered for the Navy in January 1955; a semi-navalised prototype (XF828) was flown on 20 June 1955 and the first of an initial production batch totalling seventy-seven Sea Vixen F(AW). Mk 1s (commencing XJ474) on 20 March 1957. The Royal Navy's first Sea Vixen unit, No. 700Y Flight, was commissioned in November 1958 for intensive flying trials, and the fighter entered service with No. 892 Squadron in July 1959. The Sea Vixen had no gun armament – the first British service aircraft to take this step – but instead, in the underside of the nose, were two retractable packs each housing fourteen 2 in. unguided Microcell rockets. There were six underwing pylons, the outer two being generally used for fuel tanks and the others carrying Firestreak or Bullpup missiles, 500 or 1,000 lb. bombs, or pods of heavier-calibre rockets. About a hundred Sea Vixen Mk 1s were built, these being joined in service from 1964 by the more advanced F(AW). Mk 2, able to carry four Red Top missiles and further distinguished by its bigger and longer fuselage booms, extending over and ahead of the wings and containing additional fuel. Production of the F(AW). Mk 2 version is not believed to have been extensive, but was augmented by the conversion of a number of Mk 1 aircraft to the later standard.

50 & 51 McDonnell Douglas F-4 Phantom II

There is nothing even remotely wraith-like about McDonnell Douglas's second Phantom, whose warload alone is greater than that of a World War 2 Lancaster or B-29. This solid, ugly interceptor, strike and reconnaissance aeroplane serves with three U.S. air arms, several other air forces, and is the subject of one of the largest post-war programmes yet, in any country; more than four thousand four hundred Phantoms had been completed by 1974. It originated to a U.S. Navy specification for a single-seat carrier-based attack fighter, and when ordered in 1954 was designated AH-1. In 1955 the U.S.N. altered its requirement to specify a missile-armed fighter, changing the designation to F4H-1. Twenty-three F4H-1s were ordered for test purposes, the first of these flying on 27 May 1958 with two J79-GE-3A engines. Evaluation of these aircraft led to a number of modifications, notably the introduction of dihedral on the outer wing panels, anhedral on the all-moving tailplane, a blown-flap system of boundary layer control and the adoption of more powerful J79 engines. The trials batch, and the first twenty-four production Phantom IIs, became F4H-1Fs when fitted with J79-GE-2 or -2A turbojets, and parallel versions were ordered by the U.S.A.F. – adopting a production Navy fighter for the first time in its history – as the F-110A and photo-reconnaissance RF-110A. In 1962, when the U.S. services adopted a unified designation system, the F4H-1F became the F-4A, the definitive F4H-1 (with J79-GE-8 engines) became the Navy/Marine Corps F-4B (six hundred and thirty-five built), the proposed F4H-1P 'camera job' became the U.S.M.C's RF-4B, and the U.S.A.F. versions became F-4C and RF-4C respectively. The U.S.A.F. eventually received five hundred and eighty-three F-4Cs, for service with Tactical Air Command, Pacific Air Force and U.S. Air Forces Europe. Thirty-six of this version were supplied to the Spanish Air Force. The first F-4C was flown on 27 May 1963; deliveries were completed in 1966, by which time 29 U.S.N. squadrons were operating the F-4B. Production of the RF-4C was continuing in 1974, by which time more than five hundred had been completed. The F-4D, first flown on 8 December 1965, was a U.S.A.F. model with J79-GE-15 engines and improved radar and electronics; eight hundred and twenty-five F-4Ds were built, sixty-four of this version being supplied to the Imperial Iranian Air Force and eighteen to South Korea. Further improvements in equipment and operational capability resulted in the F-4E, a multi-role version for the U.S. Air Force first flown on 30 June 1967. This has more powerful J79-GE-17 engines, a permanent installation of an M61 20 mm. multi-barrel cannon under the nose and extra fuel capacity. It has been exported to Greece (thirty-six), Iran, Israel and Turkey (forty), and Mitsubishi is building one hundred and twenty-eight for the Japan Air Self-Defence Force. The RF-4E is a multi-sensor reconnaissance version ordered originally by Federal Germany (eighty-eight), and which flew for the first time in October 1970. Japan has ordered fourteen of these as the RF-4EJ, and others have been ordered by Iran. Israel has ordered one hundred and sixty-eight F-4Es and RF-4Es. The F-4F is a version with leading-edge slats for the German Luftwaffe, which has ordered a hundred and seventy-five.

The first updated model for the U.S. Navy was the F-4G, an interim F-4B conversion which entered service in the Vietnam theatre in 1966. A more extensive F-4B conversion is the F-4J for the U.S. Navy and Marine Corps (F-4H not being used to avoid confusion with the original F4H-1). Powerplant of the F-4J is the J79-GE-10; other improved features include drooping ailerons and slotted tail, to reduce landing speed, Doppler fire control radar and other equipment changes. First flight of an F-4J was made on 27 May 1966. Beginning in 1973, a further one hundred and seventy-eight F-4Bs were being updated in a later programme, under the designation F-4N.

Two 'Anglicised' versions of the Phantom are also in service, following 1964–65 decisions to adopt the type for the Royal Navy and R.A.F. respectively. Both are powered by Rolls-Royce Spey turbofan engines, and have the American designations F-4K and F-4M. The F-4K is based on the F-4B airframe, but has a foldable nose, wider air-intake ducts, reduced tailplane anhedral, modified and strengthened landing gear and Martin-Baker ejection seats. Original orders were for two YF-4Ks (the first of which was flown on 27 June 1966), two F-4Ks and twenty-four FG. Mk 1s. Deliveries began in April 1968, but owing to changes in British naval aviation policy only one operational Fleet Air Arm squadron – No. 892 – was equipped with the type; the remaining FG. Mk 1s were transferred to the R.A.F. The F-4M is basically similar, retaining the folding wings and arrester gear of the F-4K, and is designated FGR. Mk 2 by the R.A.F. It flew for the first time on 17 February 1967; deliveries began in August 1968, the first R.A.F. squadrons equipped with the FGR. Mk 2 being Nos. 6 and 54 of Air Support Command.

52 & 53 Aeritalia (Fiat) G91 and G91Y

Overcoming strong French competition in the 1954 contest to find a standard tactical fighter for N.A.T.O., the first of three prototype G91s (4,050 lb. = 1,837 kg. st Bristol Orpheus B.Or. 1 engine) was flown on 9 August 1956. The modified second and third machines were powered by 4,850 lb. (2,200 kg.) st Orpheus 801 engines. Twenty-seven pre-production G91s, with pointed noses, began to join the 103rd Light Tactical Fighter Group of the Aeronautica Militare Italiano from August 1958, and in 1964 sixteen of these aircraft, with guns deleted and underwing smoke canisters added, were modified as G91PAN for the Pattuglia Acrobatica Nazionale, Italy's national aerobatic team, who call their mounts Frecce Tricolori (the three-coloured arrows).

The two basic service versions of this design by Giuseppe Gabrielli were the G91R single-seat reconnaissance-fighter, and the tandem 2-seat G91T combat trainer/tactical fighter; both have a blunt nose housing three aerial cameras. Early deliveries to the Italian Air Force included twenty-four each of the G91R/1 and R/1A (improved navigation equipment), and fifty G91R/1Bs, with four 0·50 in. Colt-Brownings and two underwing pylons each with a maximum 250 lb. (113 kg.) load of bombs or rockets. These were joined by one hundred and one four-gun G91T/1 operational trainers. Major user, however, was the Federal German Luftwaffe, with three hundred and forty-four G91R/3s (fifty built by Fiat, two hundred and eighty-two built and twelve assembled by Dornier, Heinkel and Messerschmitt); fifty Italian-built G91R/4s originally ordered under a U.S.A.F. contract and intended for Greece and Turkey, with twin 30 mm. DEFA cannon in place of the machine-guns; and forty-four Fiat-built and twenty-two Dornier-built G91T/3s. The German R/4s were subsequently transferred to the Portuguese Air Force. Luftwaffe G91Rs have four wing pylons, carrying 500 lb. (227 kg.) on each inner and 250 lb. (113 kg.) on each outer one. Variants designated G91R/5 and R/6 were projected but not built.

The G91Y, first details of which were announced in the spring of 1965, was developed from the G91 as a single-seat tactical fighter-bomber and reconnaissance aircraft. It is based substantially upon the airframe of the 2-seat G91T, but has twin afterburning jet engines mounted side by side in the fuselage. This arrangement provides some 60 per cent more thrust than in the single-engined G91, enabling the G91Y to carry a much-enhanced payload of weapons and/or fuel and to cruise, if required, with one engine shut down. Two prototypes were ordered in 1965, these being converted from G91Ts and making their first flights on 27 December 1966 and in September 1967. They were followed in July 1968 by the first of twenty pre-production aircraft, and the Aeronautica Militare Italiano has since placed orders for forty-five production G91Ys. There is provision for JATO rockets to halve the normal take-off distance, and an arrester hook for use under SATS (Short Airfield for Tactical Support) conditions. The G91Y has a fixed installation of three cameras and two 30 mm. DEFA cannon in the nose, and four underwing stations for 4,000 lb. (1,814 kg.) of ordnance including bombs, pods of seven 2 in., twenty-eight 2 in. or four 5 in. rockets, or 750 lb. (340 kg.) napalm containers.

54 McDonnell F-101 Voodoo

Although its production ended in 1961, the Voodoo was still operational with some units of the U.S. Air Force, the Canadian Armed Forces and the Chinese Nationalist Air Force a decade later. It had its origins in the XF-88, which was flown in 1948 and cancelled two years later; this project was revived in 1951 and, with many design changes and a fresh powerplant, ordered as a long-range escort fighter for Strategic Air Command. When S.A.C. lost interest in 1954 it was adopted as a tactical fighter-bomber by Tactical Air Command, for whom the single-seat F-101A entered service in May 1957. First flight was made on 29 September 1954, by one of twenty-nine F-101As ordered in 1952. Forty-eight additional F-101As (J57-P-13 engines) were followed by forty-seven F-101Cs, a strengthened version for low-level close support duties with four 20 mm. cannon and provision for a tactical nuclear weapon on a central pylon. T.A.C. also received, in even greater numbers, unarmed reconnaissance counterparts to both of these models, thirty-five RF-101As (plus two YRF-101A prototypes) and one hundred and sixty-six RF-101Cs being built altogether. These had two cameras installed in the centre fuselage and four others in a lengthened nose. Twenty-five of the RF-101Cs were supplied to Nationalist China. In October 1965 three squadrons of T.A.C. aircraft were transferred to the Air National Guard for conversion to RF standard (currently RF-101G and H), and the RF-101As and Cs of T.A.C. began to be supplanted in 1965 by the RF-4C Phantom II. A 2-seat all-weather interceptor version, the F-101B, flew for the first time on 27 March 1957 and entered service with Air Defense Command of the U.S.A.F. in 1959. The F-101B was powered by J57-P-55 engines and, instead of a cannon armament, carried three Hughes Falcon air-to-air missiles on a rotating ventral bay, and two Douglas Genie nuclear missiles externally. Four hundred and eighty were built, including a number of TF-101B dual-control trainers for the U.S.A.F., and fifty-six CF-101Bs and ten CF-101Fs (with dual controls) for the R.C.A.F. In 1971 the surviving Canadian CF-101s were exchanged for sixty-six ex-U.S.A.F. F-101Bs, given the new designations F-101F and TF-101F in Canadian service.

55 HAL HF-24 Marut (Wind Spirit)

India's first home-produced jet fighter, and the first non-Soviet supersonic fighter to be developed in any Asian country, the Marut was a long time in reaching service status. It was conceived by a team under the noted German designer Dr Kurt Tank, and was designed to perform ultimately at Mach 2, although a suitable powerplant has yet (1974) to be found. The Brandner E-300 engine evolved for the Egyptian HA-300 fighter was flown in an HF-24 airframe on 29 March 1967, but the cancellation of the HA-300 programme in May 1969 ended the possibility of the Egyptian engine being used to power the Indian fighter. More recently under consideration have been the Turboméca Adour and the Turbo-Union RB.199 turbofans. Kurt Tank's single-seat HF-24 prototypes (two were built) had twin Orpheus 703s mounted side by side in the rear fuselage, the first machine (BR-462) making its maiden flight on 17 June 1961 and the second (BR-463) on 4 October 1962. They were preceded on 21 March 1959 by the first of many test flights with an unpowered full-size wooden model of the aircraft. Hindustan Aeronautics is building the Mk I ground attack fighter with the Orpheus 703, following eighteen pre-production Maruts, the first of which (BD-828) was flown in April 1963. Delivery of four aircraft was made in May 1964, and in all twelve of the pre-production aircraft were delivered to the Indian Air Force. The first full-production Mk I was flown on 15 November 1967, and about a hundred had been built by early 1974, these serving with Nos. 10 and 220 Squadrons of the I.A.F. From the forty-first aircraft onwards, all Maruts have a 10 per cent increase in wing chord over the whole span. Armament of the Marut Mk I consists of four 30 mm. Aden cannon in the nose, and a rectractable under-fuselage pack of fifty 68 mm SNEB air-to-air rockets; for the strike role, these can be augmented by four rocket pods, napalm canisters, 1,000 lb. bombs or drop-tanks. Variants include the Mk IT tandem 2-seat trainer, the first example of which (BD-888) made its first flight on 30 April 1970. The two prototypes are being followed by about ten production Mk ITs. Four pre-production Mk IIs were ordered in 1973, and these will have an HAL-developed afterburner fitted to their Orpheus engines. Dr Tank and the German members of the design team left HAL in 1967, since when development of the HF-24 has been continued by an all-Indian team under the leadership of Mr S. C. Das.

56 Vought F-8 Crusader

Nearly two decades after its first flight (25 March 1955), the Crusader can still claim uniqueness for its two-position variable-incidence wing, which hinges upwards to give more lift for take-off, more drag for landing, while keeping the fuselage parallel to the deck to maintain a good view from the cockpit. The F-8A and F-8B (corresponding to the former F8U-1A and F8U-1E) were day fighter versions. Three hundred and eighteen F-8As were built, delivery beginning in March 1957 to U.S.N. Squadron VF-32 (U.S.S. *Saratoga*). This version has now been relegated to a training role as the TF-8A. Production of the F-8B totalled one hundred and thirty. The photographic RF-8 – which, as the F8U-1P, did much of the necessary reconnaissance during the 1962 Cuban crisis – remained operational with the U.S. Navy and Marine Corps in 1974. Production of RF-8As totalled one hundred and forty-four, of which fifty-three were modified in 1965–1966, and a further twenty later, to RF-8G standard with strengthened wings and fuselage, twin ventral fins and an improved camera installation. Subsequent versions included the day-fighter F-8C (J57-P-16 engine, one hundred and eighty-seven built), the F-8D limited all-weather fighter (one hundred and fifty-two, with J57-P-20 engines), and the F-8E with full all-weather ability; of this last version, a total of two hundred and eighty-six were completed. This figure does not include forty-two F-8E(FN) for the French Aéronavale; these have a blown-flap system and equip Flottilles 12F and 14F on board the carriers *Clémenceau* and *Foch*, having been modernised to F-8J standard since their first entry into service. In addition to the RF-8G conversions, a further modification programme has concerned the modernisation of three hundred and seventy-three F-8D, E, C and B aircraft to become, respectively, F-8H (eighty-nine), F-8J (one hundred and thirty-six), F-8K (eighty-seven) and F-8L (sixty-one). This programme, completed in 1970, chiefly involved modifications aimed at extending the service life of the airframe, updating the avionics and improving mission capability. The first conversion, an F-8H, flew for the first time on 17 July 1967.

All Crusaders, except the RF-8A/G, have four 20 mm. Colt cannon in the nose, and can carry two or four Sidewinders on the fuselage sides. There are underwing points for two Bullpup missiles, two 2,000 lb. or more smaller bombs, or twenty-four Zuni rockets, for attack missions. The French Crusaders have provision to carry Matra R.530 missiles instead of Bullpups.

57 Vought A-7 Corsair II

The Corsair II (in fact the third Vought aeroplane to bear the name), visibly declaring its descent from the F-8 Crusader, was the winner of four competing designs to meet a U.S. Navy requirement, outlined in 1963, for an attack aircraft to succeed the McDonnell Douglas Skyhawk in the late 1960s. In the event the Skyhawk has continued to flourish, but this has not prevented the Corsair II from being manufactured in substantial numbers, both for the U.S.N. and the U.S. Air Force. The Corsair lacks the Crusader's variable-incidence wing, and has a non-afterburning engine, since only a subsonic performance was required; but it has a greater range than the Skyhawk and can carry up to 15,000 lb. (6,804 kg.) of externally-mounted rockets, bombs and missiles on six underwing pylons and two stations on the fuselage sides. The early models also had a built-in 20 mm. gun armament in the front of the fuselage.

The first of seven evaluation A-7s was flown on 27 September 1965, and four of these were delivered to the U.S. Naval Air Test Center at Patuxent River in September 1966, as A-7As. Ling-Temco-Vought subsequently built one hundred and ninety-nine of the A-7A version (TF30-P-6 engine), deliveries of which were completed in the spring of 1968. The first operational A-7A unit was Squadron VA-147, which commissioned in February 1967 and went into action (from the U.S.S. *Ranger*) in the Vietnam theatre in the following December. The A-7B was a developed version, with uprated TF30-P-8 engine giving 12,200 lb. (5,534 kg.) thrust; one hundred and ninety-six were built, the first one flying on 6 February 1968 and the last being delivered in April 1969. The TF30-P-8 also powered the first two examples of the A-7D, the first of which flew on 6 April 1968, but the three hundred and eighty-seven production A-7Ds ordered up to 1974 are fitted with 14,250 lb. (6,465 kg.) st TF41-A-1 turbofans, a version of the Rolls-Royce Spey built by Allison Motors. The first TF41-powered A-7D was flown on 26 September 1968, and deliveries began three months later. These are employed in the fighter/strike role by the U.S.A.F's Tactical Air Command, whose first formation to equip with the A-7D was the 54th Tactical Fighter Wing. The two 20 mm. cannon of the original models are replaced in the A-7D by a single Vulcan M-61A1 multi-barrel 20 mm. cannon, installed in the port side of the lower front fuselage. In July 1969 deliveries began to the U.S. Navy of the A-7E, which is essentially similar to the A-7D and has more advanced avionics than earlier U.S.N. models. This version entered operational service in 1970 with VA-146 and VA-147 (U.S.S. *America*). By early 1974, A-7E orders for the U.S. Navy totalled four hundred and eighty-eight aircraft, of which the first sixty-seven have TF30-P-8 turbojet engines (and are thereby designated A-7C to avoid confusion) and the remainder have 15,000 lb. (6,804 kg.) st TF41-A-2 turbofans. A further sixty have been ordered by Greece.

Projected versions of the Corsair II have included the unbuilt KA-7F refuelling tanker; the A-7G, similar to the A-7D but with an uprated Spey engine, put forward as a potential Hunter replacement for the Swiss Air Force; and the tandem 2-seat YA-7H, first flown on 29 August 1972. This is a private-venture prototype operational trainer. No orders had been placed for it by late 1974, but eighty-one A-7B/C are to be converted to 2-seat configuration and designated TA-7C.

58 BAC Lightning

The twin-engined BAC (originally English Electric) Lightning, which has been the R.A.F's front-line fighter for more than a decade, was also the first British-designed combat aircraft capable of a Mach 2 performance. Stemming from the English Electric P.1A, which was first flown on 4 August 1954, the Lightning also owed much to research carried out, from 1952, with the Short S.B.5. Two Sapphire-engined P.1As (WG760 and WG763) were built, followed by three P.1B prototypes (XA847, XA853 and XA856, first flight 4 April 1957) with Avon engines and twenty development aircraft (XG307-313 and XG325-337). Initial production version was the F. Mk 1, first flown (XM134) on 29 October 1959 and delivered to No. 74 Squadron of R.A.F. Fighter Command (as it then was) from the summer of 1960. Armament consisted of two 30 mm. Aden cannon and two Firestreak air-to-air missiles. The generally similar F. Mk 1A, with in-flight refuelling capability, equipped Nos. 56 and 111 Squadrons. Twenty F. 1s and twenty-eight F. 1As were built. From the Mk 1A were developed the F. Mk 2 (fourteen built) and F. Mk 2A (thirty converted from F. Mk 2), with longer range, improved reheat system and later avionics, the first example of which (XN723) was flown on 11 July 1961. These three early production models all had the original form of round-topped fin. First model with the now-standard square-topped fin, of greater area, was the F. Mk 3, which flew for the first time (development aircraft XG310) in November 1961 and in definitive production form (XP693) on 16 July 1962. Powered by 16,360 lb. (7,420 kg.) st Avon 300-series engines, sixty-three F. 3s were built, entering service from April 1964 with Nos. 23, 29, 56, 74 and 111 Squadrons. Armament of the Mks 2 and 3 consisted of two Hawker Siddeley Red Top missiles in lieu of Firestreaks, the gun armament being deleted. On 17 April 1964 the prototype (XP697) was flown of the F. Mk 6, a fully-developed version of the Mk 3 of which sixty-two were completed with cambered, less-sweptback outer wings, a ventral fuel/weapons pack of more than double the capacity of that first introduced on the Mk 3, and provision for an arrester hook for short-field landings. The large overwing fuel tanks first tested on the Mk 3 became standard on the Mk 6, which was delivered to Nos. 5, 11, 23 and 74 Squadrons beginning in December 1965. R.A.F. operational trainer versions, corresponding to the Mks 1 and 3 fighters respectively, are designated T. Mk 4 and T. Mk 5, and have side by side 2-seat cockpits with modified canopies in a wider front fuselage. There were two T. 4 prototypes (XL628 and XL629) and twenty production aircraft; a production T. 4 (XM967) served as prototype for the twenty-two production T. Mk 5s.

Exports of the Lightning have included five F. Mk 2 and two T. Mk 4 aircraft supplied in 1966–67 as F. Mk 52/T. Mk 54 to the Royal Saudi Air Force, and the F. Mk 53 and T. Mk 55 special export models ordered by both Saudi Arabia and Kuwait. First flights were made on 1 November and 3 November 1966 respectively by the first F. 53 (53–667) and first T. 55 (55–710) for the R.S.A.F.; deliveries to Saudi Arabia, which ordered thirty-four Mk 53s and six Mk 55s, began later in December 1967. Kuwait's order was for twelve F. 53s and two T. 55s. The F. Mk 53 is a developed version of the R.A.F. Mk 6, with Avon 302-C engines and multi-mission capability. The ventral tank can house two 30 mm. Aden guns in place of some of the fuel; forward of the tank is a weapon bay which can accommodate various mission packs comprising two Firestreak or Red Top missiles, forty-four 2 in. unguided rockets, five reconnaissance cameras or night reconnaissance equipment. Each of the two underwing pylons can carry a pair of 1,000 lb. high-explosive, retarded or fire bombs, two launchers for eighteen 68 mm. rockets apiece, two flare pods or two machine-gun pods. The two overwing pylons can each carry a 260 gallon (1,182 litre) auxiliary fuel tank for ferry purposes.

59 Dassault Mirage F1

The Mirage F1, which entered service with the Armée de l'Air in 1973, owes its origin to a contract placed with Dassault by the French government in 1964 to develop a replacement for the Mirage III multi-purpose combat aircraft. The prototype built to meet this requirement, the Mirage F2, was designed as a 2-seat low-altitude 'penetration' fighter to be powered by a single Pratt & Whitney TF306 turbofan engine. In the event this engine was not available in time for the F2's first flight, which was made on 12 June 1966 under the power of a TF30 engine instead. Despite the retention of the Mirage name, the new aircraft was considerably larger and heavier than the Mirage III, and had sweptback tapered wings and tailplane instead of a tail-less delta configuration.

No further examples of the F2 were built, Dassault having predictably won favour instead for the F1, which it developed in parallel with the F2 as a private venture. This is much closer in size to the Mirage III (using a scaled-down version of the F2 wing), is a single-seater, can use – initially, at least – the same weapons systems as the Mirage III-E, and is powered by the SNECMA Atar 9K engine already well proven in earlier Mirages. The private-venture prototype was lost in a crash on 18 May 1967, but had performed well enough since its first flight on 23 December 1966 for the French government to order three pre-production F1s and a structural test airframe. The first pre-series Mirage F1 flew on 20 March 1969, the second on 18 September 1969, and the third on 17 June 1970. By mid-1974 one hundred and five production aircraft (first example flown on 15 February 1973) had been ordered for the Armée de l'Air, and others by the air forces of Greece (forty), Kuwait (twenty), South Africa (forty-eight) and Spain (fifteen). Initial production version is the F1-C all-weather interceptor; Dassault has also projected an F1-A 'utility' version and an F1-B two-seat operational trainer. Deliveries of the F1-C began on 20 December 1973 to the 30e Escadre de Chasse at BA.112, Marin la Meslée, near Reims. Three Armée de l'Air Escadres are to be equipped with the F1-C, of which the second is the 5e Escadre at Orange.

Production F1s are being manufactured in association with SABCA and Fairey in Belgium. Initially they are being powered by the Atar 9K-50 engine, but plans are to fit two aircraft with the more powerful M53 Super Atar once this engine is suitably developed, permitting an increase in maximum high-altitude speed from Mach 2·2 to Mach 2·5. An M53-engined prototype (designated F1-E) is scheduled to fly in 1975. The Mirage F1-C has a fixed armament of two 30 mm. DEFA 553 cannon in the lower front fuselage, provision for a Matra 550 or Sidewinder missile at each wingtip, and one under-fuselage and four underwing strongpoints for additional stores. Alternative external loads can include up to three Matra 530 radar or infra-red homing missiles; two more Matra 550s or Sidewinders; one Matra/HSD Martel missile; one Aérospatiale AS.30 missile; eight 450 kg. bombs; four launchers containing eighteen rockets each; two Dassault CC.420 or similar gun pods; one reconnaissance pack; or six 300 litre (66 Imp. gallon) or three 1,200 litre (264 Imp. gallon) drop-tanks.

60 Dassault Mirage G8

The swing-wing Mirage G-01 prototype, built to a French government contract placed in October 1965, flew for the first time on 18 November 1967, and completed more than four hundred hours of successful test flying before being lost in a crash on 13 January 1971 following an electrical system failure. This aircraft is the subject of the illustration. Although nominally a research aircraft, the Mirage G-01 originated as an all-French parallel to the since-abandoned Anglo-French variable-geometry fighter project. It was a 2-seat aircraft, with a single Pratt & Whitney TF306 afterburning turbofan engine and wings whose sweep could be varied between 20 degrees (fully forward) and 70 degrees (fully swept). It was capable of Mach 2·5 at altitude, and was supersonic at ground level. The fuselage, engine installation and tail unit were broadly similar to those of the fixed-wing Mirage F1 (*q.v.*).

In September 1968 the French government ordered two further prototypes, slightly larger than the original aircraft, powered by two SNECMA Atar 9K-50 turbojet engines and designated Mirage G4. Budgetary considerations led later to these being redesigned as much smaller and lighter aircraft, designated G8. They made their first flights on 8 May 1971 and 13 July 1972, the first G8 being a 2-seater and the second a single-seater. Atar 9K-50 engines (15,873 lb. = 7,200 kg. st with afterburning) are installed in these initially, but later the aircraft will be powered by 18,740 lb. (8,500 kg.) st SNECMA M53 Super Atar turbojets. The Mirage G8 has a maximum take-off weight in the region of 44,100 lb. (20,000 kg.), nearly 20 per cent lower than that of the G4. Equipment includes Cyrano IV multi-purpose radar and a low-altitude navigation/attack system incorporating Doppler radar, a laser rangefinder and bombing computer.

The Mirage G8A is a developed version of the G8, to be used in the ACF (Avion de Combat Futur) programme to evolve a successor to the Mirage F1.

61 SEPECAT Jaguar

By no means the 'poor man's Phantom' that some once claimed it to be, the Franco-British Jaguar is the first major fixed-wing combat aircraft to be designed, developed and manufactured on a fully-international basis. The airframe is the product of collaboration between the Dassault–Breguet group in France and British Aircraft Corporation, the powerplant is the Rolls-Royce/Turboméca Adour turbofan engine, and overall responsibility for the Jaguar programme is vested in the Société Européenne de Production de l'Avion E.C.A.T. (SEPECAT). This company was formed in May 1966, a year after the signing of a project agreement between the French and British Defence Ministries. Development was begun of three basic versions: a single-seat tactical support version (Jaguar A for the Armée de l'Air, first flown on 29 March 1969, and Jaguar S for the R.A.F., first flown on 12 October 1969); single-seat carrier-based tactical version (Jaguar M for the Aéronavale, first flown on 14 November 1969); and 2-seat advanced (Jaguar E for France) or operational (Jaguar B for Britain) training versions. Eight flying prototypes were built, comprising two each of the A, E and S versions and one each of the Jaguar M and B. First Jaguar to fly, on 8 September 1968, was the E-01 prototype; the eighth (the B-08) flew for the first time on 30 August 1971. Development of the naval version was halted in 1973, despite a successful flight test programme. The Anglo-French agreement calls for two hundred Jaguars to be built for each country, of which (up to the Spring of 1974) firm contracts had been placed for two hundred and seventy-eight (eighty Jaguar As and forty Es for France; thirty-seven Bs and one hundred and twenty-one Ss for Britain). The remainder were expected to be ordered by the end of that year. R.A.F. designations are GR. Mk 1 for the single-seat Jaguar S and T. Mk 2 for the 2-seat Jaguar B.

All versions of the Jaguar have a fixed armament of two 30 mm. DEFA 553 or Aden cannon in the underside of the fuselage, except for Jaguar B, which has one Aden. The tactical versions have one under-fuselage and four underwing weapon stations, capable of carrying a maximum load of 10,000 lb. (4,500 kg.) of bombs, rockets, Martel anti-radar missiles or drop-tanks. Jaguar A can carry an AN52 tactical nuclear weapon. An air-to-air missile (Sidewinder or later type) can be fitted at each wingtip, and provision is made for in-flight refuelling of the single-seat versions. The 2-seat versions both have a secondary strike capability and can carry similar weapon loads.

Deliveries of production aircraft began in 1973, France's 7e Escadre de Chasse being the first to receive them, with the delivery of A and E Jaguars in mid-year to Escadron 1/7 'Provence' at Base Aérienne 113 at Saint-Dizier. The R.A.F. received its first Jaguar GR. Mk 1s in May and September 1973, for ground crew and flying training respectively at the Operational Conversion Unit at Lossiemouth. First operational R.A.F. Jaguar squadron, No. 54, was formed on 29 March 1974, to be followed by No. 6 Squadron and eventually by six additional operational Jaguar squadrons.

An International Jaguar, with uprated engines and other options, is available for export. First customers were Oman and Ecuador, each of which ordered twelve in the late summer of 1974.

62 Mitsubishi T-2 and FS-T2-KAI

First flown in prototype form (19-5101) on 20 July 1971, the Mitsubishi T-2 (XT-2 is the prototype designation) is a supersonic jet trainer for the Japan Air Self-Defence Force, and is being developed under contract from the Japan Defence Agency. Design work, under the leadership of Dr Kenji Ikeda, was completed in 1968 and was followed in 1969 by the production of a full-size mockup. The T-2 bears a strong external resemblance to the Anglo-French Jaguar, and that similarity is enhanced by the fact that both aircraft are powered by two Adour turbofan engines. Its primary role will be to provide transition training for J.A.S.D.F. pilots flying the F-104J Starfighter or F-4EJ Phantom, both of which Mitsubishi has manufactured in Japan. Four prototypes and a structural test airframe have been built, and an initial production contract for twenty T-2s was placed in March 1973. A further twenty-two were ordered a year later. The T-2, which is due to begin entering service in 1975, is Japan's first nationally-developed supersonic aircraft, and Fuji, Nippi and Shin Meiwa are major sub-contractors for production aircraft.

The proposed FS-T2-KAI is a single-seat close-support fighter version, retaining the 20 mm. Vulcan multi-barrel cannon of the T-2 and having four underwing attachments and one on the fuselage centre-line for up to twelve 500 lb. bombs, two or four infra-red air-to-air missiles, two air-to-surface missiles, or other external loads. These hardpoints are also present, for armament training loads, on the T-2. Twenty-two FS-T2-KAI (service designation F-1) are to be purchased initially.

63 Republic F-105 Thunderchief

Hailed on its appearance as 'the world's most powerful one-man aeroplane' and as 'a re-usable missile', the Thunderchief is indeed large for a single-seat aircraft and can carry a frightening array of internal and external weapons. Last design by the Republic Aviation Corporation before it became a Division of Fairchild Hiller Corporation in mid-1965, the Thunderchief was initiated as a private venture, receiving official support when an evaluation batch of fifteen aircraft was ordered by the U.S.A.F. in 1954. These were completed as two YF-105As, three RF-105Bs (later redesignated as special-test JF-105Bs) and ten F-105Bs. The YF-105As, the first of which (54–0098) was flown on 22 October 1955, were powered by Pratt & Whitney J57-P-25 engines pending availability of the definitive engine, the more powerful J75. The latter engine was fitted to the first F-105B, which flew on 26 May 1956 and introduced such major design changes as an area-ruled fuselage and swept-forward air intakes. A further sixty-five true production F-105Bs followed, having J75-P-5 engines instead of J75-P-3s. Deliveries, to squadrons of the 4th Tactical Fighter Wing of the U.S.A.F., began in May 1958. At that time the F-105B, which could carry 8,000 lb. (3,630 kg.) of bombs internally and a further 4,000 lb. (1,814 kg.) externally, was the heaviest single-seater ever to enter U.S.A.F. service. However, only three T.A.C. squadrons were equipped with the F-105B day fighter-bomber, as this was quickly superseded in production by the all-weather F-105D, which became the major service version.

A more powerful engine, the 26,500 lb. (12,030 kg.) st J75-P-19W, was installed in the F-105D, whose versatility was increased by the ability to carry its entire 12,000 lb. weapon load externally if required, provision for four Sidewinder air-to-air or Bullpup air-to-surface missiles, and more sophisticated avionics including an air data computer, Doppler navigation system, a toss-bombing computer and N.A.S.A.R.R. search and ranging radar. As in the F-105B, an M61 Vulcan 20 mm. multi-barrel cannon is installed in the forward fuselage. The first F-105D was flown on 9 June 1959. It entered production shortly afterwards, and deliveries to Tactical Air Command began in May 1960. Six hundred and ten F-105Ds were built, eventually equipping more than thirty U.S.A.F. squadrons. In 1970 some thirty F-105Ds were being modified to carry a newly-developed bombing system called T-Stick II; these aircraft are identifiable by a deep 'saddleback' dorsal spine fairing from the cockpit to the fin. An operational trainer version, the F-105F, was ordered in 1962. This has a 2 ft. 7 in. (0·79 m.) longer fuselage, to accommodate a second cockpit in tandem, and fin height and area is increased compared with the F-105D. The first F-105F flew on 11 June 1963, and one hundred and forty-three were completed before production ended in 1964, bringing total manufacture of Thunderchiefs, including prototypes, to eight hundred and thirty-three. By the late 1960s the F-105B model had been withdrawn to units of the Air National Guard, but both the F-105D and F-105F continued to be used extensively in the Vietnam campaigns until 1973, and were subject to various equipment modernisation programmes.

64 Hawker Siddeley Harrier

Combining a performance better than that of the Hunter with the ability to take off and land vertically on almost any solid surface, the Harrier has completed more than five years service as the world's first and only fixed-wing operational combat aeroplane with VTOL capabilities. Originating as a private venture, the first P.1127 prototype made its initial vertical take-off on 21 October 1960, and its first transition from hovering to forward flight some eleven months later. After six prototype P.1127s, Hawker Siddeley built nine Kestrel F(GA). Mk 1s (first example flown on 7 March 1964) which, between April and November 1965, were thoroughly tested in Britain by a three-nation squadron of pilots from the R.A.F., the Federal German Luftwaffe, and the U.S. Army, Navy and Air Force. In February 1965 production was authorised of six Harrier development aircraft for the R.A.F. (first flight 31 August 1966): subsequent R.A.F. orders have totalled ninety-two of the single-seat close support/tactical reconnaissance version and thirteen of the 2-seat operational training version. First flights by the GR. Mk 1 and T. Mk 2 were made on 28 December 1967 and 24 April 1969; the former version entered service with Air Support Command on 1 April 1969 – the 51st anniversary of the R.A.F.'s formation – and was followed by the T. Mk 2 in 1970. In 1974 Harriers equipped Nos. 1, 3, 4 and 20 Squadrons in the U.K. and Germany. In May 1969 four Harriers took part in the *Daily Mail* trans-Atlantic air race, being refuelled in flight by Victor tanker aircraft. One, flown by Sqn. Ldr. T. Lecky-Thompson, forms the subject of the colour plate: it set a world record flight time of 5 hr. 57 min. for the 3,490 mile (5,615 km.) journey between the centres of London and New York. The 2-seat Harrier differs from the single-seat model primarily in having a new, longer nose section, to accommodate two cockpits in tandem, enlarged fin surfaces, and a lengthened tail cone. Both models have the same weapons capability, attachment points under the wings (four) and fuselage (two) permitting the carriage of various combinations of gun pods, bombs, rockets and flares; a reconnaissance-camera pod can be carried on the fuselage centreline pylon. There is no built-in armament. R.A.F. Harriers are cleared for operation with a maximum load of 5,000 lb. (2,268 kg.). They have undergone progressive in-service improvement, first to GR. Mk 1A/T. Mk 2A standard by installing the 20,000 lb. (9,072 kg.) st Pegasus Mk 102 engine in place of the 19,000 lb. (8,618 kg.) Mk 101 originally fitted; and currently to GR. Mk 3/T. Mk 4 standard by replacing the former engine by the 21,500 lb. (9,752 kg.) st Pegasus Mk 103. A laser rangefinder, specified for the GR. Mk 3, is installed in a new 'thimble' nose fairing. Hawker Siddeley operates a 2-seat Harrier Mk 52 demonstrator (G-VTOL), which is essentially similar to the T. Mk 4.

The Pegasus 103 engine (U.S. designation F402-RR-401) is also installed in the Harrier Mk 50 export version, ordered by the U.S. Marine Corps as the single-seat AV-8A (one hundred and two) and 2-seat TAV-8A (eight). The first ten AV-8As were delivered, in 1971, initially with Pegasus 102s, but were later brought up to Pegasus 103 standard. U.S. Harriers are in service with three Marine Corps squadrons (VMA 231, 513 and 542) in North and South Carolina. The Spanish Navy has ordered, through the U.S. Navy, six AV-8As and two TAV-8As.

In mid-1974 the future was under review of two new Harrier developments. Of these, the Maritime Harrier for the Royal Navy seemed certain to be shelved, at least for the present. The Advanced Harrier (AV-16A), of which the U.S.M.C. wants three hundred and forty-two to succeed the AV-8A in the early 1980s, is planned to have a new-concept wing and a 25,000 lb. (11,340 kg.) st Pegasus 15 engine, giving it twice the weapons payload/combat radius capability of the AV-8A; but without adequate British government support it is likely to be undertaken largely, if not entirely, by McDonnell Douglas and Pratt & Whitney, with the original airframe and engine design companies relegated to the role of minor sub-contractor.

65 Convair F-102A Delta Dagger

The F-102A, which entered service with the U.S.A.F. in 1956, can trace its history back to the small, delta-winged XF-92A which first flew on 18 September 1948. When, two years later, the U.S.A.F. issued a specification for a supersonic interceptor, the basic concept of the XF-92A was scaled up to yield the YF-102. The first of ten YF-102s made its maiden flight on 24 October 1953, but was patently incapable of exceeding Mach 1 and for a time its future seemed in jeopardy. Successful application of the area rule principle to the aircraft's body, however, resulted in the YF-102A (four built) which first flew on 20 December 1954 and fully met the U.S.A.F.'s requirements; and the long and satisfactory service given by the eight hundred and seventy-five F-102As subsequently built more than vindicated the aircraft's uncertain start. The first fifty-three F-102As had a somewhat smaller fin and rudder. A further sixty-three aircraft were built as 2-seat TF-102A combat proficiency trainers (first example flown on 8 November 1955), fully capable of normal operational missions. Production was completed in April 1958. Both models were modernised while in service, with more advanced electronics for greater efficiency at all altitudes, and in-flight refuelling. The first gun-less U.S. interceptor, the Delta Dagger carries four Hughes Falcon air-to-air missiles and twenty-four 2·75 in. folding-fin unguided aerial rockets. It has full all-weather capability, and served with the U.S. Air Forces Europe, the Pacific Air Force and Air Defense Command units in the U.S.A. By 1973 it no longer equipped front-line U.S.A.F. units, but nine fighter-interceptor groups of the Air National Guard still operated the type, and others have been supplied to the air forces of Greece and Turkey.

66 General Dynamics (Convair) F-106 Delta Dart

Close family resemblance between the Dart and Dagger is no coincidence, for the F-106 began its development period in 1955 as the F-102B version of the Delta Dagger. Such were the ultimate differences between the two, however, that an entirely new F designation was allotted. Apart from the obvious external variations – the slimmer fuselage, re-sited intakes and swept vertical tail surfaces – the F-106 has half as much power again as the earlier Dagger and even after a decade and a half of service it is still one of the most advanced interceptors flying. The Delta Dart's electronic guidance and fire control equipment, designed to work with the SAGE (Semi-Automatic Ground Environment) defence system, detects its target by radar and launches its four Falcon and/or two Genie missiles entirely automatically. If need be, an entire combat mission, between take-off and touchdown, can be flown without the pilot touching a single control. The first Delta Dart to fly, on 26 December 1956, was a production F-106A. Two hundred and seventy-seven single-seat F-106As and sixty-three 2-seat

F-106B combat trainers (first flight 9 April 1958) had been built when production ended late in 1960. First deliveries were made in July 1959, and by the middle of 1961 Delta Darts equipped about half the all-weather squadrons of the U.S.A.F.'s Air Defense Command. Various improvements made during service have included the installation of zero-height crew escape systems and provision for underwing drop-tanks and in-flight refuelling capability. In 1970 tests were conducted with an F-106A (58-795) fitted with an improved-visibility cockpit hood, optical gun-sight and an M-61A 20 mm. multi-barrel cannon installed in a semi-retractable under-fuselage fairing. This gun installation was adopted as a standard fit for in-service aircraft in 1973.

67 Saab 35 Draken (Dragon)

The Draken story goes back as far as 1949, to a time when no other delta-winged aircraft had been flown, and only the rocket-powered Bell X-1 had exceeded Mach 1, let alone approached Mach 2. Under Saab's chief designer, Erik Bratt, Project R1250 was begun in August 1949 to meet the most demanding specification ever issued by the Royal Swedish Air Force. After three years' intensive design study a small research aircraft, the Saab 210, powered by a 1,100 lb. (500 kg.) st Armstrong Siddeley Adder turbojet engine, flew on 21 January 1952 to pioneer Saab's unique double-delta wing form, and in August 1953 a contract was placed for three prototype Saab 35s and three pre-production Saab 35As. The first Saab 35 flew on 25 October 1955. The J 35A was the initial production model, of which sixty-five were built, the first of them entering service with F13 late in 1959. A number of these were converted to SK 35C 2-seat operational trainers, which first flew on 30 December 1959 and entered Flygvapnet service in 1960. The J 35B, first flown on 29 November 1959, was slightly longer, had a modified cockpit canopy and Saab S7 collision course radar; both it and the J 35A were powered by the Swedish-built RM6B (Avon 200) engine, delivering 15,200 lb. (6,895 kg.) st with afterburning, and were armed with four 30 mm. cannon and four Sidewinders, rocket pods or 250 kg. bombs. Increased engine power – the RM6C (Avon 300) – and more advanced electronics were introduced with the J 35D, which flew for the first time on 27 December 1960, entered production in 1962 and service in 1963. Most J 35As and Bs were later converted to this standard. The S 35E, a tactical reconnaissance counterpart to the J 35D, was first flown on 27 June 1963 and began to enter service late in 1964. The final Flygvapnet model, the J 35F, first flew (as a converted D) early in 1961. The J 35F has an improved S7B fire control system; it has a single 30 mm. Aden M/55 cannon in the starboard wing, and carries externally four Hughes Falcon radar-guided (RB327) or infra-red (RB328) homing weapons. It entered service in 1966, and production of all these models has now ended. From the J 35D onwards all Drakens have a performance above Mach 2, as well as excellent short-field characteristics, a high rate of roll, tight turning radius and a rate of climb at sea level, with afterburning, of 34,450 ft. (10,500 m.) per minute.

In mid-1967 Saab announced the Saab 35X (for Export), with increased internal fuel capacity and external weapons load, as a tactical strike and reconnaissance aircraft. During 1968 the Danish Defence Ministry placed two contracts for a total of forty Saab 35XDs and six (later increased to eleven) 2-seat Saab 35XT trainers. The first Saab 35XD was flown on 29 January 1970, and this version is known as the F-35 (fighter/bomber) and RF-35 (reconnaissance/fighter) by the Flyvevåben, which has twenty of each; the 2-seat version has the trainer/fighter designation TF-35. First R.D.A.F. unit to receive Drakens was No. 725 Squadron at Karup. Finland's Ilmavoimat is to have twelve similar Saab 35XS (=Export Suomi), ordered in April 1970 for delivery 1974–75. These are being built under licence in Finland by Valmet, and were preceded by the lease of six Saab 35Bs from Sweden for familiarisation purposes. The total number of Drakens built or on order for Sweden, Denmark and Finland amounts to more than six hundred.

68 Saab 37 Viggen (Thunderbolt)

The Viggen, named after the thunderbolt or hammer of Thor, is scheduled by the mid-1970s to have replaced the Lansen and Draken in the roles of attack and reconnaissance. Saab's canard layout, with its anhedral mainplane and smaller, no-dihedral, flap-equipped foreplane, is a bold but logical design, and the Viggen's appearance, apart from the wing arrangement, is not unlike the American Phantom, which the Swedish government studied closely before deciding to pursue the native design. This was evolved during 1952–58 by a team led by Erik Bratt (also responsible for the Draken), though the final design was not 'frozen' until May 1963. The canard layout is, in effect, a variation on the 'double-delta' concept embodied in the Draken, and enables the Viggen to retain virtually the same excellent STOL performance as its predecessor while operating at significantly greater combat weights at all levels and possessing a superior rate of climb. The first of seven prototype/pre-production Viggens was rolled out in November 1966 and made its first flight on 8 February 1967. The first six aircraft, all of which were single-seaters, were flying by April 1969, and were followed on 2 July 1970 by the seventh aircraft, the prototype for the SK 37 2-seat operational training version. By 23 February 1971, when the first production Viggen flew, orders had been placed for one hundred and seventy-five Viggens, these comprising the AJ 37, an all-weather attack aircraft with secondary capability as an interceptor, and the SK 37. In fact, the development and service introduction programme has proceeded so well that the same funds will now cover the production of an additional five aircraft. The AJ 37 entered service with F7 at Satenäs in mid-1971 to replace the A 32A Lansen; first SK 37 deliveries were made in June 1972. Later versions include the interceptor/attack JA 37 (thirty ordered); the tactical reconnaissance SF 37, intended to replace the S 32C Lansen; and the SH 37 armed sea surveillance version, to replace the S 35E Draken. The SF 37 was flown for the first time on 21 May 1973. To power the Viggen, Volvo (formerly Svenska) Flygmotor AB developed the Pratt & Whitney JT8D-22 civil turbofan engine to deliver some 26,450 lb. (12,000 kg.) of thrust, and service aircraft have RB04 or RB05 air-to-surface missiles as primary armament in the attack role. There are altogether seven permanent stores points beneath the fuselage and wings, with provision for two extra underwing points if required. These can also carry a wide variety of air-to-surface rockets, bombs, 30 mm. Aden guns or mines; air-to-air missiles for the interception role; or camera or radar pods for reconnaissance. A miniaturised digital computer, using a memory unit with an eight-thousand-word 'vocabulary', provides automated navigation, target location and fire control, integrated with Sweden's STRIL 60 ground defence network as well as being able to fly the aeroplane automatically. Like its predecessors in service, the Viggen will operate from Sweden's underground hangar system (the tail fin folding down for indoor stowage) and be able to take off from any 500 m. (1,640 ft.) stretch of straight trunk road.

69, 70 & 71 **Dassault Mirage III and Mirage 5**
The little MD 550 Mirage I first flew on 25 June 1955; the larger and much-modified Mirage III prototype which followed it on 17 November 1956 has since yielded a supremely versatile family of warplanes capable of high- or low-level interception in all weathers, nuclear strike, tactical reconnaissance and strike, and combat training, in addition to experimental VTOL and swing-wing derivatives. Ten pre-production Mirage III-As were built, powered by an Atar 9B engine and with provision for an SEPR 841 rocket motor; the first one was flown on 12 May 1958. The first series-built single-seat model was the Mirage III-C interceptor/attack aircraft, with a generally similar powerplant and Cyrano I*bis* nose radar. First flight of a III-C was made on 9 October 1960, and about a hundred and fifty-five were subsequently built for the Armée de l'Air. A 2-seat operational trainer equivalent is the Mirage III-B (first flight 21 October 1959). The

major production model is the Mirage III-E, which is a longer-range tactical strike version with a more powerful Atar 9C turbojet engine, optional SEPR 844 rocket motor and Cyrano II radar. One hundred and eighty of this version were built for the Armée de l'Air, the first production III-E being flown on 14 January 1964. Trainer equivalent of this is the III-BE: French Air Force orders for the B and BE totalled forty. A tactical reconnaissance version of the III-E is the Mirage III-R, externally recognisable by its snub nose, in which are installed three oblique and two vertical cameras. The prototype first flew on 31 October 1961, and the first of fifty III-Rs and twenty III-RDs for the Armée de l'Air was flown on 1 February 1963.

These, together with the 2-seat Mirage III-D, are the basic production models of the Mirage III. Large numbers have been built for, or in, nearly a dozen countries outside France, and are identified by suffix letters added to the basic designation. Customers include Argentina (twelve III-EA and two III-DA); Australia (two pattern aircraft from France, followed by fifty ground-attack III-OA, forty-eight III-OF interceptors and ten III-D trainers built by Commonwealth Aircraft Corporation and the Government Aircraft Factories, and a further six III-Ds from France); Brazil (twelve III-EBR and four III-DBR); Israel (seventy-two III-CJ and three III-BJ); the Lebanon (twelve III-EL and two III-BL); Libya (thirty III-ED and ten III-RD); Pakistan (eighteen III-EP, three III-DP and three III-RP); South Africa (sixteen III-CZ, three III-BZ, sixteen III-EZ, three III-DZ and four III-RZ); Spain (twenty-six III-EE and four III-DE); Switzerland (one III-C, two III-BS, thirty-six III-S built locally by FFA, and eighteen III-RS); and Venezuela (nine III-EV).

In the ground attack role the Mirage III-E normally carries two 30 mm. DEFA cannon in the fuselage, an AS.30 air-to-surface missile or two 450 kg. bombs under the fuselage, and similar-sized bombs, rockets or drop-tanks beneath the wings. For interception duties the built-in guns are optional, and one Matra R.530 missile and two Sidewinders can be carried.

On 19 May 1967 Dassault flew the prototype of a less-sophisticated version, the Mirage 5. This is based on the airframe and powerplant of the Mirage III-E, but has simplified avionics and seven external stores points giving a greater capacity for fuel and weapon carriage. This can reach 8,820 lb. (4,000 kg.) of weapons and 220 Imp. gallons (1,000 litres) of fuel in ground attack configuration, and the aircraft can also be operated as an interceptor. Orders for the Mirage 5 up to mid-1974 included twelve 5-AD/5-RAD and two 5-DAD for Abu Dhabi; sixty-three 5-BA, twenty-seven 5-BR and sixteen 5-BD for Belgium; fourteen 5-COA, two 5-COR and two 5-COD for Colombia; sixty 5-D/5-DE/5-DR and ten 5-DD for Libya; twenty-eight 5-PA for Pakistan; twenty 5-P and two 5-DP for Peru; thirty-four 5-SDE and four 5-SDD for Saudi Arabia; four 5-V and two 5-DV for Venezuela; and fifteen 5-M/5-DM for Zaïre. Fifty Mirage 5-Js ordered by Israel were embargoed by the French government and later allocated to the French Air Force with the designation Mirage 5-F. Total Mirage III and Mirage 5 orders at mid-1974 were thus in the region of one thousand three hundred.

In mid-1968 Dassault began developing a further member of the Mirage family, known originally as the Milan (kite). This has retractable foreplanes (called 'moustaches') to improve low-speed handling and operation from short airstrips with steep approaches. The first fully-representative Milan was flown on 29 May 1970, powered by a 15,875 lb. (7,200 kg.) thrust Atar 9K-50 afterburning engine. The 'moustaches' are available as an optional fit for all Mirage III and Mirage 5 variants.

72, 73 & 74 Mikoyan MiG-21 ('Fishbed')

Undoubtedly one of the most extensively-built and widely-used combat aircraft in the world today, the MiG-21 is in service in several versions with the Soviet Air Force and more than a score of associate countries. It was first seen by western observers at the June 1956 Aviation Day display at Tushino, when two slightly differing E-5 prototypes made their appearance. First flown in 1955, these aircraft subsequently received the N.A.T.O. reporting names Fishbed-A and Fishbed-B. The first standard production model was the MiG-21F (Fishbed-C), the suffix letter indicating a more powerful engine than that fitted to the prototype and pre-production aircraft. The MiG-21F has been supplied, in varying quantities, to the air forces of Afghanistan, Algeria, the Chinese People's Republic, Cuba, Czechoslovakia, Egypt, Finland, the German Democratic Republic, Hungary, India, Indonesia, Iraq, North Korea, Poland, Romania, Syria and Yugoslavia. This version has been or is being built in China and Czechoslovakia. The MiG-21F is a short-range clear-weather day interceptor, armed with either one or two 30 mm. NR-30 cannon in the underside of the nose and a K-13 'Atoll' infra-red homing missile or a pod of sixteen 57 mm. rockets beneath each wing. There is a third stores attachment point beneath the fuselage, usually occupied by an auxiliary fuel tank to offset the MiG-21F's modest internal fuel load. A tandem 2-seat trainer version is designated MiG-21UTI and bears the N.A.T.O. code name 'Mongol-A'. The MiG-21F has been followed into service in some countries by an improved version designated MiG-21PF (Fishbed-D), the 'P' suffix letter denoting an all-weather version of the earlier model. This type has a more powerful RD-11 engine, and is distinguishable by its less-tapered nose, larger-diameter air intake and much larger centre-body radar, broader-chord fin (on most aircraft), a fairing aft of the cockpit and other detail changes. No fixed gun armament is fitted, but pods of sixteen 57 mm. rockets may be alternated with Atoll missiles on the underwing pylons. Fishbed-Ds have been supplied to Bulgaria, Egypt, East Germany, Hungary, Poland and North Vietnam. Further Soviet development has yielded versions known as Fishbed-F (MiG-21PFM), Fishbed-H (MiG-21R and RF), Fishbed-J (MiG-21PFMA and MiG-21MF), and Fishbed-K. Main external differences between Fishbed-F and -D are the former's broader fin, sideways-hinged cockpit canopy, and, on some aircraft, a brake parachute 'acorn' at the base of the fin and dielectric aerial fairing at the top of the fin. A version of the Fishbed-F, built in Czechoslovakia, is designated MiG-21SPS and is fitted with blown flaps. Fishbed-H is a tactical reconnaissance version of Fishbed-J, able to carry camera or other sensor pods and ECM equipment; Fishbed-K is also similar to the J but carries wingtip ECM pods and has a longer dorsal spine. The version identified as Fishbed-J was first seen when it began to equip Soviet Air Force units stationed in Egypt in 1970. It has a strengthened wing structure, which gives it supersonic capability at sea level. It incorporates all or most of the improved features of the Fishbed-F and has a deeper, straight-topped dorsal spine fairing. Moreover, it has a multi-mission capability, the number of underwing attachments being increased to four, on which interception and/or ground-attack weapons may be carried. Late-production models have a 23 mm. twin-barrel GSh-23 cannon mounted in an under-fuselage fairing. The latest known version (up to spring 1974) was the MiG-21MF Fishbed-K, distinguishable by its constant-depth dorsal spine and more powerful RD-13 engine. Two-seat variants of the broad-finned MiG-21s are code-named Mongol-B.

Chinese production of the MiG-21, as the Shenyang F-8, is undertaken without a licence. It began with the Fishbed-C model, but has been updated by reference to Fishbed-D and more advanced versions as they staged through the country en route to North Vietnam and North Korea. Up to 1974 production in China is not thought to have been extensive – possibly of the order of about a hundred aircraft. More legitimately, HAL in India imported ten MiG-21Fs and two MiG-21PFs in 1963–64, following these with the licence production of one hundred and ninety-six Indian-built PFs before proceeding in 1973 to production of the PFMA version, of which a hundred and fifty have been ordered by the Indian Air Force. The IAF also received forty-two

Mongols, mostly of the B versions.

The basic MiG-21 design has also yielded a number of experimental or record-breaking aircraft, beginning with the E-66, a modified MiG-21F which set up a world speed record in 1959 of 1,484 m.p.h. (2,388 km./hr.). The same aircraft, its turbojet assisted by a 6,615 lb. (3,000 kg.) st rocket motor, became the E-66A which reached a record height of 113,892 ft. (34,714 m.) in April 1961. Soviet women pilots have established several closed-circuit speed records in the E-76, basically similar to the MiG-21PF, and in the E-33, equivalent to the MiG-21UTI. At the Aviation Day display in 1967, the U.S.S.R. showed a STOL version of the MiG-21PF (code name Fishbed-G), with a wide-track main landing gear and two vertically-mounted lift-jet engines beneath an upward-opening door in the centre of a lengthened fuselage. At least one MiG-21, with tailplane deleted and a new, ogival-planform wing, was used to provide aerodynamic data in the development programme for the Tu-144 supersonic airliner.

75 Sukhoi Su-9 and Su-11 ('Fishpot')

A contemporary of the MiG-21 day interceptor, Pavel Sukhoi's Su-9, with its Su-7B stablemate, revealed the first major application by the U.S.S.R. of the design practice of 'commonality'; that is, to reduce the cost of developing two entirely different aeroplanes to fulfil two distinct functions, they were instead designed in parallel to bear certain features and components in common with one another. Thus, while these two fighters share the same basic fuselage and tail assembly, the Su-7B ground-attack aircraft employs a sharply-swept and tapered thin-section wing whereas the Su-9 all-weather interceptor has a thicker wing and follows a 'tailed delta' configuration. The Su-9 prototype (Fishpot-A) was first exhibited publicly in 1956. It had a 'chin' type intake beneath the radar nose-cone, and was armed with two 30 mm. cannon in the wing roots. Fishpot-B, the first production model, had a fully-circular intake, incorporating the radome as a conical centrebody, and the wing-root guns were deleted in favour of four underwing 'Alkali' radar homing missiles for the interception role. Complementing the MiG-21 by providing all-weather point defence in the Russian homeland, the Su-9 was built only for use within the Soviet Union, and is probably no longer in production. It has been in Soviet Air Force service since about 1959. The record-breaking T-431 of 1959 was almost certainly an Su-9 or a derivative. A more recent version of the aircraft in service, as demonstrated at Domodedovo in 1967, has a longer, less-tapered nose and twin dorsal strakes similar to those of the Su-7BM, an enlarged centrebody radome, and can carry two 'Anab' (infra-red or semi-active radar homing) missiles beneath the wings. This has been identified as the Su-11 Fishpot-C. The tandem 2-seat trainer version of the Su-9 has the N.A.T.O. code name 'Maiden'. The Su-9 and Su-11 began to be joined in service by the Su-15 Flagon-A during the late 1960s.

76 Sukhoi Su-15 ('Flagon-A')

Among the new combat aircraft displayed by the Soviet authorities at Domodedovo Airport in July 1967 was a twin-jet single-seat all-weather interceptor fighter emanating from the Sukhoi design collective and allocated the N.A.T.O. code name Flagon-A. Ten of these aircraft – a formation of nine and an all-black singleton – appeared in the fly-past, from which it was evident that the new fighter was a much-developed derivative of the single-engined Su-9. The wings in particular are closely similar to those of the Su-9, and there is an obvious family resemblance in the tail units of the two types. The fuselage, however, is some 20 per cent longer, housing two side-by-side afterburning turbojets, each of comparable thrust to the Su-9's single engine, and incorporating a large dielectric nose radar fairing. A wide-track tricycle landing gear is fitted, as on the Su-9, and association with the earlier type is strengthened by the presence of two large, door-type air-brakes on each side of the rear fuselage. The Su-15 is reported to have entered Soviet Air Force service in 1968, presumably as an eventual replacement for the slower Su-9, and about 400 were thought to be in service by mid-1971, with production continuing. The Su-15s exhibited in 1967 revealed no gun armament, but had a stores point beneath each outer wing panel to carry 'Anab' air-to-air missiles – one infra-red homing type and one radar homing type. There were two side-by-side attachment points beneath the centre of the fuselage, on which additional weapons or auxiliary fuel tanks could be carried.

Also in 1967 the U.S.S.R. exhibited a single prototype of a basically similar aircraft modified for STOL operation. This was code-named Flagon-B, but is thought to have been no more than a research aircraft, though its modified wing planform has been seen on non-STOL Su-15s in service, which have the code name Flagon-C. This wing has decreased sweep on the outer leading-edges, the overall span being thereby extended to about 35 ft. 0 in. (10·65 m.). The Flagon-B's centre fuselage was widened slightly aft of the cockpit to accommodate three vertically-mounted lift-jet engines. These were installed in tandem beneath two upward-opening intake doors and exhausted via louvres in the underside of the fuselage, between the intake trunks for the propulsion engines.

77 Yakovlev Yak-28P ('Firebar')

The first production Soviet warplane designed from the outset as a radar-equipped night and all-weather fighter was the Yak-25 ('Flashlight-A'), a 2-seat swept-wing aircraft powered originally by AM-5 engines and later, in its Yak-25F form, by two, 5,512 lb. (2,500 kg.) st Klimov RD-9 non-afterburning turbojets. It entered service in late 1955 and was a relatively unsophisticated design compared with contemporary western types. The improved Yak-25R Flashlight-B and Yak-27 Flashlight-C appeared at Tushino in 1956; the latter did not go into widespread service, but the Yak-25R, a ground attack version with glazed nose and other refinements, did become operational, as did the modified Yak-26 'Mangrove' tactical reconnaissance version.

In 1961 a trio of Yak-25 derivatives appeared in the air display at Tushino. These were all, initially, thought to be fighter variants, and were coded Firebar-A, -B and -C respectively. The -A and -C versions were later classified as light bombers under the code name 'Brewer', now known to be the Yak-28, and are described in the companion to this volume. Firebar, in whose designation the suffix letter P indicates an all-weather interceptor version of the basic Yak-28, thus represents the third phase in the 'stretch' of the original Yak-25, although it is almost entirely a new aeroplane. A barely supersonic performance (Mach 1·1) was achieved by further modifying and increasing the area of the wings, raising them at the same time to shoulder level; by installing higher-powered engines with reheat; by increasing fin height and area; and by a general improvement in aerodynamic quality. In recent years the nose has been further modified, to accommodate an even longer radome. The armament consists of two 'Anab' air-to-air homing missiles, one carried beneath each wing outboard of the engine nacelle. There is no built-in armament. The performance of the Yak-28P, which has been in Soviet Air Force service since the early 1960s, still does not represent a major improvement over the later Yak-25 models, and would probably be effective only against targets flying at subsonic speeds. On the other hand, it doubtless inherited from its predecessor a useful climb rate and bad-weather capability which may offset deficiencies in other directions. A dual-control trainer version, with an extra, stepped-down cockpit canopy in front of the normal one, has the code name 'Maestro'.

78 Tupolev Tu-28P ('Fiddler')

The allocation of an 'F' code name indicates that, as far as western circles are concerned, the Fiddler is regarded basically as a fighter aircraft. However, the use of the designation suffix letter P usually indicates an all-weather interceptor *version* of the basic design, and it seems likely that Fiddler was designed as a multi-purpose combat aeroplane. The bulk and weight of the Tu-28P is clear from its landing gear – twin nosewheels and four-wheel main units, the latter retracting into bullet-shaped housings that project from the trailing edge of the wing. Twin afterburning turbojets are mounted in the rear fuselage, their long, shoulder-mounted intake ducts commencing just aft of the cockpit and forming part of the general area-ruling of the aircraft's body. The Tu-28P's size should allow for a generous fuel load, giving it the range to intercept, outside Soviet territory, attackers carrying stand-off bombs, or to carry out tactical strike or reconnaissance missions. As an all-weather interceptor, the Tu-28P has a standard armament of a pair of 'Ash' missiles (one each of the infra-red homing and radar homing type) beneath each outer wing panel, but it is possible that other weapons may be carried. The Tu-28P, which carries a two-man crew, has been in squadron service with the Soviet Air Force at least since the beginning of 1963, following the public showing of two prototypes at the Tushino air display two years earlier. The design is clearly derived from that of the experimental Tu-98 'Backfin' prototypes flown in 1955, but the large ventral bulge and two undertail fins seen in 1961 do not appear on later aircraft in service.

79 **Mikoyan MiG-25 ('Foxbat')**
In 1965 the U.S.S.R. received official confirmation of a new world record for speed over a 1,000 km. (621 mile) closed circuit by an aircraft which it identified as an 'E-266'. This aircraft, piloted on that occasion by Alexander Fedotov, had flown at 1,441·5 m.p.h. (2,320 km/hr.) at an altitude of 69,000–72,000 ft. (21,000–22,000 m.), carrying a payload of 4,409 lb. (2,000 kg.). Two years later, at the Aviation Day display at Domodedovo, near Moscow, four E-266s taking part gave western observers their first glimpse of this large twin-engined, single-seat military aeroplane, which the commentator described as 'high altitude all-weather interceptors' with a Mach 3 performance. Design of the aircraft, now identified as the MiG-25, was probably aimed originally at producing an air superiority fighter, perhaps as a counter to America's SR-71A strategic reconnaissance aircraft and XB-70 Valkyrie strategic bomber, both capable of Mach 3 flight. Further evidence of the Foxbat's capabilities was given on 5 October 1967, when a 2,000 kg. payload was carried to a height of 98,349 ft. (29,997 m.) and a 500 km. (310 mile) closed-circuit speed of 1,852·61 m.p.h. (2,981·5 km/hr.) was attained on further record flights; and on 27 October 1967, when the 1,000 km. record of 1965 was raised to 1,814·81 m.p.h. (2,920·67 km/hr.). A further crop of records in 1973 included two for payloads of 1,000 kg. and 2,000 kg. to an altitude of 115,583 ft. (35,230 m.), and climbing times of 2 min. 49·8 sec. to 65,617 ft. (20,000 m.) and 4 min. 3·86 sec. to 98,425 ft. (30,000 m.).

Such achievements confirm beyond question the Foxbat's very high performance; yet not until

1971 did firm evidence begin to appear regarding its service status, and, even some ten years after its design was initiated, much information regarding the MiG-25's combat potential remains speculative. It has been described by the U.S. Secretary of the Air Force as 'probably the best interceptor in production in the world today' (1973), and is believed to be in service in two versions. The interceptor has four underwing hardpoints for air-to-air missiles, probably of the 'snap-down' type, and there is a bulge under the forward part of each intake trunk which may enclose a gun or other armament. The version used for high altitude reconnaissance is distinguished by a slightly longer, camera-packed nose (with no dielectric covering over the nose radar) and tail-fins which have broken taper on their trailing edges. It is presumably unarmed, although the underwing hardpoints are retained.

The first reports of operational MiG-25s appeared in the spring of 1971, when Soviet Air Force squadrons equipped with them were airlifted into Egypt. These were later withdrawn, but Foxbats have since been reported in other Middle Eastern theatres of conflict.

80 Mikoyan MiG-23 ('Flogger')

At the 1967 Aviation Day display at Domodedovo Airport, near Moscow, examples were shown of two single-seat prototype aircraft featuring variable-geometry or 'swing' wings: the Sukhoi Su-7E and Mikoyan MiG-23. Both have since entered production and service, the former as the 2-seat Su-17 (NATO code name 'Fitter-B') and the latter as 'Flogger-B' and in 2-seat form as the MiG-23U. Powered by a single large afterburning turbojet engine, the Mikoyan Flogger-A prototype of 1967 was credited by the official commentator at Domodedovo with a Mach 2 capability at medium and high altitudes, and bore a general resemblance in size and configuration to the contemporary French Dassault Mirage G-01 prototype. The Mikoyan fighter is believed to have entered production in about 1970-71, and by mid-1971 there was evidence that it had begun to enter Soviet Air Force service. Subsequently, reports appeared of its presence in Egypt, East Germany and Syria, and in 1974 the publication of photographs of the 2-seat MiG-23U enabled a more up-to-date appraisal to be made of the two versions currently in service.

These indicate that the Flogger is a slightly smaller aircraft than was at first thought, and probably has a rather less powerful engine. They also reveal a number of new or revised features compared with the Flogger-A prototype. The basic wing geometry appears to be comparatively little changed, there being some 21 degrees of leading-edge sweep in the fully-forward position, increasing to 71 degrees when fully swept. There is, however, some suggestion of a change in the location of the wing pivot points, and of some reduction in wing aspect ratio, possibly resulting from the provision on production aircraft of leading-edge slats on the outer two-thirds of the moving panels of the wings. The all-moving tailplane is mounted high on the fuselage, slightly below the line of the wings, and the gap between this and the trailing-edge of the fully-swept wing has apparently been reduced in comparison with the Flogger-A. Ample keel area is provided by a large main fin with a generous dorsal fairing (larger still on the MiG-23U), and by a ventral fin beneath the tailpipe, the lower portion of this fin folding sideways to starboard to give ground clearance when the landing gear is down. The two lateral airbrakes below the tailplane have apparently been retained. There are five attachments for external stores, three under the fuselage and one beneath the wing glove box on each side. Ahead of the fuselage hardpoints is a fairing housing the Flogger's fixed armament, a single twin-barrel gun for close-range fighting, most probably the same 23 mm. GSh-23 weapon that is fitted to the MiG-21MF.

81 General Dynamics F-111

Winner of the U.S. Defense Department's 1961 TFX (Tactical Fighter Experimental) competition, the 'swing-wing' F-111 had an extremely unhappy development and early service career. A Senate investigating sub-committee, reporting early in 1971, found that five major errors of judgement had been made, including the very decision to start the TFX programme and the selection, in November 1962, of the second-best (yet more expensive) aircraft proposed. As a result, the report continued, the sum of money spent to acquire about five hundred F-111s was greater than that estimated as the cost of more than *seventeen* hundred originally required – and that, of those five hundred, less than one hundred approached the required technical or operational standard.

Twenty-three evaluation aircraft were procured originally, comprising eighteen F-111As for the U.S.A.F. and five F-111Bs, with a shorter nose and extended-span wings, for the U.S. Navy. However, the naval version persistently proved overweight for its carrier-based fleet defence fighter role, and the F-111B programme was cancelled in mid-1968 after only two additional examples had been completed.

Meanwhile evaluation of the F-111A, first flown on 21 December 1964, was followed by one hundred and forty-one production examples, delivery of which began in 1967 to the 474th Tactical Fighter Wing at Nellis A.F.B., Nevada. Six of these aircraft made a disastrous start to the aeroplane's operational career when, within five days of their first combat sorties in Vietnam, two of their number were lost. A reconnaissance version of the F-111A, designated RF-

111A, was flown for the first time on 17 December 1967. Two aircraft, part of a cancelled British requirement for fifty F-111Ks, were assigned to the U.S.A.F. as YF-111As for experimental duties. The F-111A itself, which became subject to high-speed, high-altitude flight restrictions, was superseded by the F-111E with modified air intakes (ninety-four built) and the F-111D with improved avionics and TF30-P-9 engines (ninety-six built).

Strategic Air Command's requirement for two hundred and ten of the FB-111A 2-seat bomber version, as an interim successor to the early B-52s and the B-58, was reduced to the acquisition of seventy-six, delivery of which began in October 1969. The two prototypes were converted F-111As, the first flight as an FB-111A being made on 30 July 1967. The FB-111A has 'Mk IIB' avionics, the longer-span wings designed for the F-111B, TF30-P-7 engines, and a maximum warload of fifty 750 lb. bombs, two carried internally and the rest on eight underwing pylons. Twenty-four basically similar F-111Cs, with TF30-P-3 engines and Mk I avionics, were built for the Royal Australian Air Force for the strike role. Delivery of these began in 1973.

Following the F-111E on the production line for the U.S.A.F. came eighty-two F-111F fighter-bombers, in which the best features of the F-111E and FB-111A are combined with more powerful TF30-P-100 engines to give a considerably enhanced performance and operating capability.

As this final version has shown, the F-111 design is capable of being a fully-viable combat aeroplane, and its unfortunate career has been more the result of mismanagement than of fundamental shortcomings in the design. It was the first combat aircraft in the world to be produced with variable-geometry wings, and also the first tactical fighter design to attempt to satisfy the joint needs of both the U.S.A.F. and the U.S. Navy. The wings, in their fully-forward position, have 16 degrees of sweep, increasing to 72·5 degrees in the fully-swept position. External loads can be carried beneath the fuselage, under the fixed portion of the wings, and beneath the outer wings on pylons which pivot, as the wings sweep back, to keep the stores aligned fore and aft in line with the fuselage.

82 Grumman F-14A Tomcat

The Tomcat, evolved in place of the cancelled F-111B for the U.S. Navy, was declared winner over four other competitors in a Navy design programme in January 1969 and is a 2-seat, multi-purpose carrier-based fighter. The first of twelve development aircraft made its maiden flight on 21 December 1970, but crashed on the landing approach after its second test flight nine days later. The crew ejected safely, and a second F-14 made its first flight on 24 May 1971. Up to mid-1974, the U.S. Navy had placed orders for three hundred and twenty-two production F-14As (sixty-seven of which had been delivered), and Iran had ordered eighty. Avionics and other features are based on those already developed by Grumman for the F-111B, and landing gear on that of the A-6 Intruder.

The F-14A has a fixed armament of one M61-A1 Vulcan 20 mm. multi-barrel cannon, with 675 rounds, in the port side of the lower front fuselage. There are recessed stations under the fuselage, and pylons beneath the fixed portion of the wings, on which can be carried six Phoenix and two Sidewinder, or four Sparrow and four Sidewinder, air-to-air missiles; or drop-tanks. The Tomcat can also be operated in the attack role, carrying various bombs or bomb-and-missile combinations up to a maximum external load of 14,500 lb. (6,577 kg.). At the time of writing the F-14A was unique among variable-geometry ('swing-wing') aircraft in having, in addition to variable-sweep wings, small movable foreplane surfaces housed inside the leading-edge roots of the fixed portions of the wings. Fulfilling a similar function to the 'moustaches' of the Dassault Milan, these can be extended forward into the airstream as the main wings swing backward, so controlling changes in the centre-of-pressure position. The wings themselves have 20 degrees of sweep when fully forward and 68 degrees when fully back.

The first operational Tomcat unit was U.S. Navy Squadron VF-1; with VF-2, this squadron flew the first operational F-14A sorties, from the U.S.S. *Enterprise*, in March 1974.

83 McDonnell Douglas F-15A Eagle

McDonnell Douglas's F-15 design was declared the winner of a U.S.A.F. competition for a new air superiority fighter, over proposals from Fairchild Hiller and North American Rockwell, in December 1969.

The Eagle is a single-seat, twin-turbofan all-weather fighter; it is armed with a built-in rapid-firing gun (initially the 20 mm. M61-A1, with 1,000 rounds) and four Sparrow and four Sidewinder air-to-air missiles. When fully developed it will have a secondary attack capability and a radar capable of detecting low-flying targets, but the basic roles are those of air-to-air interception, fighter sweep, escort and combat air patrol. Particular emphasis has been placed, in the design of the F-15, on the dog-fighting aspects of manoeuvrability and acceleration – an area in which the gap between U.S. and the latest Soviet fighters has widened appreciably in recent years. Initial funding covered the production of twenty development aircraft (including two 2-seaters), and the first of these (71-0280) was flown for the first time on 27 July 1972, followed by the first 2-seat TF-15 on 7 July 1973. Eight Eagles had been delivered by the end of 1973, the remaining twelve development aircraft were due for delivery by the end of 1974, and the first Eagles were due to be delivered to U.S.A.F. Tactical Air Command in November 1974. The U.S. Air Force plans an eventual purchase of seven hundred and forty-nine Eagles, of which one hundred and sixty-four production aircraft (including TF-15s) had been ordered by autumn 1974. The 2-seat version is under consideration for reconnaissance and attack roles, as well as for training. Up to 12,000 lb. (5,443 kg.) of external ordnance could be carried.

84 **Hawker Siddeley Dominie**
For most of the years since the end of World War 2, the navigators of the Royal Air Force's bomber squadrons received their specialist training aboard the lumbering piston-engined Varsity; but there arose an ever-increasing gap between the flying speeds of the Varsity and successive generations of R.A.F. bombers. To close this gap the Dominie, which can fly at speeds of up to Mach 0·8, was ordered in September 1962 and entered service in 1966 with No. 1 Air Navigation School at Stradishall. Twenty of these aircraft were built for Flying Training Command (now Training Command). The Dominie is based on, and constructionally differs little from, the Hawker Siddeley 125 business jet transport, the chief outward difference being the enlarged ventral bulge, which in the Dominie houses the aerials of its Decca and Doppler navigational equipment.

The first production Dominie T. Mk 1 (XS709) was flown on 30 December 1964; the manufacturer's designation is HS 125 Series 2. Internally the Dominie is fitted out for a crew of two, one instructor and two (exceptionally three) trainees. It is not so uneconomical as it may appear to use an aeroplane of the Dominie's size to train only two men at a time, for the R.A.F. considers that in this way it can give more individual – and therefore more effective – tuition than in the 'flying classroom' type of trainer where no individual pupil has total responsibility for navigating the aircraft. From the flying viewpoint the Dominie is said to handle very well, as might be expected of an aircraft which, in all its forms, has already sold well over three hundred examples for executive use and to other equally discerning operators. The Royal Air Force also has four Hawker Siddeley 125 Series 400s (CC. Mk 1) and two Series 600s (CC. Mk 2), which serve in the communications role with No. 32 Squadron. Other air forces to employ variants of the HS 125 include those of Argentina (Navy, one), Brazil (eleven, one of which is used for calibration duties), Ghana (one), Malaysia (two) and South Africa (seven, known as the Mercurius in S.A.A.F. service).

85 **Rockwell (North American) T-39 Sabreliner/Sabre**
Although preceding Britain's Hawker Siddeley Dominie by several

years, the Sabreliner fulfils a similar function with the U.S. forces and both aircraft follow a twin rear-jet layout. The NA-246 Sabreliner was developed as a private venture to a U.S.A.F. specification for a utility aircraft and 'combat readiness' trainer, to have a performance akin to that of the Sabre fighter – hence its name. The Sabreliner prototype (N4060K) was flown on 16 September 1958, and the first T-39A on 30 June 1960, deliveries to the U.S.A.F. Air Training Command beginning later the same year. These had Pratt & Whitney J60-P-3 turbojet engines, compared with the 2,500 lb. (1,134 kg.) General Electric J85 engines of the prototype. One hundred and forty-three T-39As were completed for the U.S.A.F., three of these being converted later to T-39F electronic warfare trainers for F-105G personnel. Six T-39Bs were completed for Tactical Air Command, with Doppler radar and N.A.S.A.R.R. (North American Search and Ranging Radar) in a modified nose and a simulated F-105D cockpit on the starboard side of the cabin, for the training of Thunderchief crews. These entered service in 1961. The U.S. Navy version, for maritime radar training, is the T-39D, of which forty-two were built, the T-39C being a project only. The CT-39E is the U.S. Navy designation for nine off-the-shelf commercial Sabreliner 40s purchased for 'rapid-response' transport of high-priority passengers, ferry pilots and cargo; five of the longer Sabre 60s have been purchased, for the same role, as CT-39Gs. The U.S. Coast Guard has ordered eight Sabre 75As for a marine pollution surveillance and search role, under the designation HT-39H. The Sabreliner (now simply called Sabre) has continued in production by Rockwell for the commercial market as an executive transport.

86 Panavia MRCA (U.K./Germany/Italy)

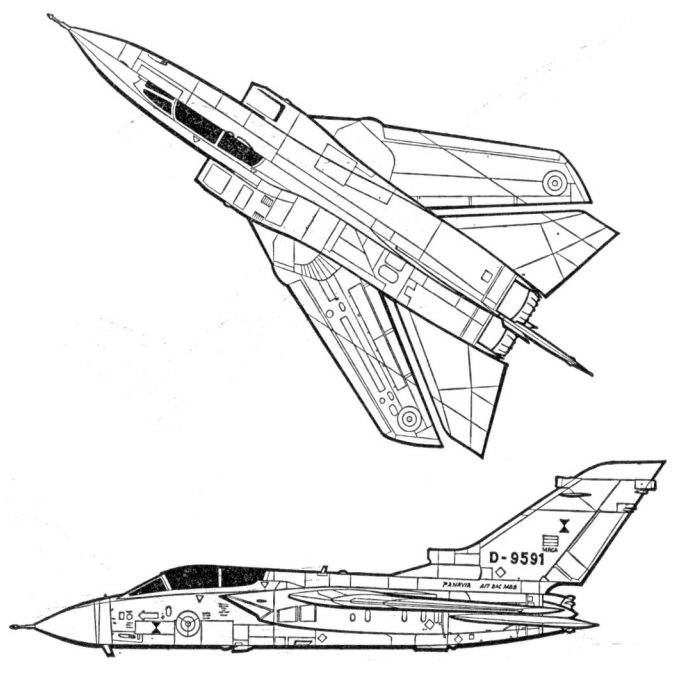

Engines: Two 8,500/14,500 lb. (3,855/6,577 kg.) st Turbo-Union RB.199-34R turbofans. *Span (spread):* 45 ft. 7¼ in. (13·90 m.) *Span (swept):* 28 ft. 2½ in. (8·60 m.). *Length:* 54 ft. 9½ in. (16·70 m.). *Height:* 18 ft. 8½ in. (5·70 m.). *Maximum take-off weight:* approx. 40,000 lb. (18,145 kg.). *Maximum speed:* more than 1,320 m.p.h. (2,125 km/hr.) at 36,000 ft. (11,000 m.). *Combat endurance (internal fuel):* approx. 1 hr. 15 min.

The 2-seat MRCA (Multi-Role Combat Aircraft) is due to enter service in 1977–78. The first of nine development aircraft (D-9591) made its first flight 14 August 1974. Orders are scheduled from the R.A.F. (three hundred and eighty-five), the Federal German Luftwaffe (two hundred and two) and Navy (one hundred and twenty), and the Italian Air Force (about one hundred). Primary roles are strike, air defence and reconnaissance; a training version will also be developed.

87 Dassault-Breguet/Dornier Alpha Jet (France/Germany)

Engines: Two 2,976 lb. (1,350 kg.) st SNECMA/Turboméca Larzac 04 turbofans. *Span:* 29 ft. 11 in. (9·12 m.). *Length:* 40 ft 3¾ in. (12·29 m.). *Wing area:* 188·4 sq. ft. (17·50 sq. m.). *Normal maximum take-off weight:* 13,227 lb. (6,000 kg.). *Maximum speed:* 602 m.p.h. (968 km/hr.) at 36,000 ft. (11,000 m.). *Service ceiling:* 49,200 ft. (15,000 m.). *Maximum range:* 1,242 miles (2,000 km.).

Developed jointly by Dassault-Breguet (the design leader) and Dornier, the 2-seat Alpha Jet will serve the French Air Force for basic and advanced training and the Luftwaffe for close support and reconnaissance, each country ordering about two hundred for service from 1976–77. Belgium is to order thirty-three trainers. Under-fuselage gun pod on German version, with bombs, rockets or drop-tanks on four underwing stations; maximum weapons load 4,850 lb. (2,200 kg.).

88 Hawker Siddeley Hawk (U.K.)

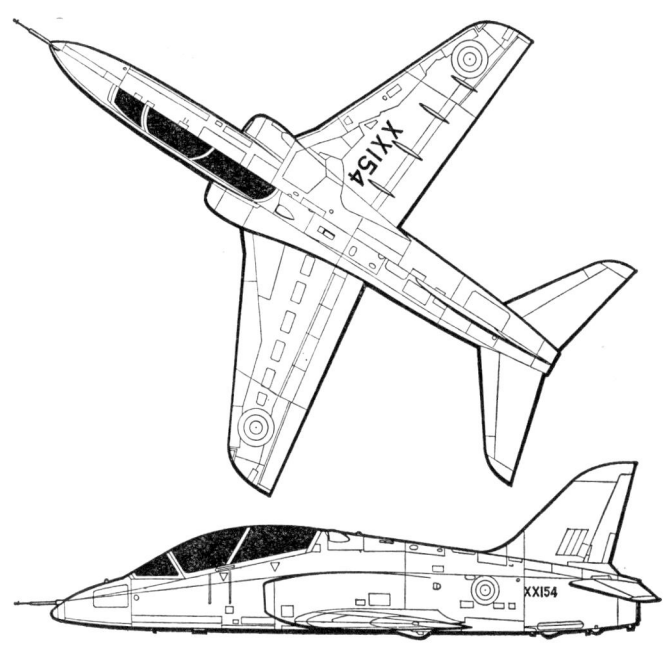

Engine: One 5,340 lb. (2,422 kg.) st Rolls-Royce/Turboméca Adour RT.176-06-11 Mk 151 turbofan. *Span:* 30 ft. 10 in. (9·40 m.). *Length, incl. nose probe:* 39 ft. 2½ in. (11·95 m.). *Wing area:* 180·0 sq. ft. (16·72 sq. m.). *Maximum take-off weight (as weapons trainer):* 12,000 lb. (5,443 kg.). *Maximum speed:* 595 m.p.h. (958 km/hr.) at 36,000 ft. (11,000 m.). *Service ceiling:* 44,000 ft. (13,410 m.). *Ferry range:* approx. 1,725 miles (2,780 km.).

One hundred and seventy-five Hawk T. Mk 1 2-seat fully-aerobatic trainers are on order for the R.A.F., for service from late 1976. They are preceded by a single prototype/pre-production aircraft, which made its first flight on 21 August 1974, and are intended to succeed the Gnat T. Mk 1. A close-support version, to carry up to 5,000 lb. (2,268 kg.) of underwing and under-fuselage weapons, is under development.

89 Fairchild A-10A (U.S.A.)

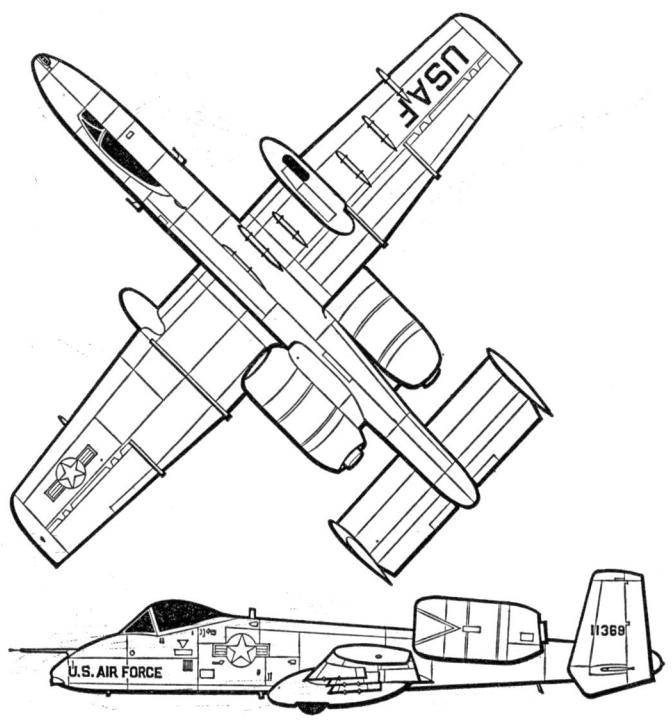

Engines: Two 9,065 lb. (4,112 kg.) st General Electric TF34-GE-100 turbofans. *Span:* 57 ft. 6 in. (17·53 m.). *Length:* 53 ft. 4 in. (16·26 m.). *Wing area:* 506·0 sq. ft. (47·01 sq. m.). *Maximum take-off weight:* 46,624 lb. (21,148 kg.) *Maximum speed (clean):* 459 m.p.h. (738 km/hr.) at sea level. *Close air support radius including 2-hr loiter:* 288 miles (463 km.).

Winner of a 1972 fly-off competition against the Northrop A-9A, the single-seat A-10A close-support aircraft flew for the first time on 10 May 1972. Six pre-production and twenty-five production examples are being built initially, with first deliveries to the U.S.A.F. scheduled for December 1975. Armament is one 30 mm. multi-barrel nose cannon and up to 16,000 lb. (7,257 kg.) of weapons on eight underwing and three under-fuselage stations.

INDEX

The reference numbers refer to the illustrations and corresponding text.

		Ref. No.	Page (colour)	Page (description)
Aeritalia (Fiat)	G91 and G91Y	52–53	67	139
Aermacchi	M.B.326	26	42	116
Aero	L-29 Delfin	27	43	117
	L-39 Albatross	28	44	118
Aérospatiale	N 262 and Frégate	13	29	106
Aérospatiale (Fouga)	Magister	20	36	111
BAC	Jet Provost and Strikemaster	31–32	47–48	120
	Lightning	58	74	144
Beechcraft	T-34 Mentor	5	21	99
Canadair	CL-41 and CT-114 Tutor	25	41	115
Cessna	T-37 and A-37	29	45	119
	T-41 Mescalero	1	17	97
Convair	F-102A Delta Dagger	65	78	151
	F-106 Delta Dart	66	79	152
Dassault	Étendard IV	43	58	130
	Mirage III and Mirage 5	69–71	82–83	155
	Mirage F1	59	73	145
	Mirage G8	60	73	146
	Super Mystère B-2	42	57	129
Dassault-Breguet/Dornier	Alpha Jet	87	—*	170
de Havilland	Vampire Trainer	34	50	123
Dornier	Do 27	2	18	97
Fairchild	A-10A	89	—*	172
FMA	I.A.35 Huanquero and I.A.50 GII	11	27	104
	I.A.58 Pucará	12	28	105
Fuji	T-1	40	55	128
General Dynamics	F-111	81	92	164
Gloster	Javelin	48	63	134

* *not in colour*

		Ref. No.	Page (colour)	Page (description)
Grumman	F-14 Tomcat	82	93	165
HAL (Hindustan Aeronautics Ltd)	HF-24 Marut	55	69	141
	HJT-16 Kiran	23	39	114
Hawker	Hunter	37–38	53	125
Hawker Siddeley	Dominie	84	95	167
	Gnat	46–47	61–62	133
	Harrier	64	77	150
	Hawk	88	—*	171
	Sea Vixen	49	64	136
Hispano	HA-200 Saeta and HA-220 Super Saeta	21	37	112
Lockheed	F-104 Starfighter	15	31	107
	T-33	19	35	111
McDonnell	F-101 Voodoo	54	68	140
McDonnell Douglas	F-4 Phantom II	50–51	65–66	137
	F-15 Eagle	83	94	166
Mikoyan/Gurevich	MiG-17	41	56	128
Mikoyan	MiG-19	44	59	131
	MiG-21	72–74	84–85	157
	MiG-23	80	91	163
	MiG-25	79	90	162
Mitsubishi	T-2 and FS-T2-KAI	62	75	148
North American	F-86D/K/L Sabre	35	51	123
	F-100 Super Sabre	36	52	124
	T-28 Trojan	6	22	100
Northrop	F-5	17	33	109
	F-5E Tiger II	18	34	110
	T-38 Talon	16	32	108
Panavia	MRCA	86	—*	169
Piaggio	P.149D	9	25	103
Republic	F-105 Thunderchief	63	76	149
Rockwell International	T-2 Buckeye	22	38	113
	T-39 Sabreliner/Sabre	85	96	167
Saab	Saab 32 Lansen	39	54	127
	Saab 35 Draken	67	80	153
	Saab 37 Viggen	68	81	154
	Saab 105	33	49	122
Scottish Aviation	Bulldog	4	20	99
	Jetstream	14	30	106
SEPECAT	Jaguar	61	74	147
SIAI-Marchetti	SF.260MX/SF.260W	10	26	103

* *not in colour*

		Ref. No.	*Page (colour)*	*Page (description)*
Soko	Galeb and Jastreb	30	46	120
	Kraguj	3	19	98
Sukhoi	Su-7 and Su-17	45	60	132
	Su-9 and Su-11	75	86	159
	Su-15	76	87	160
Tupolev	Tu-28P	78	89	161
Vought	A-7 Corsair II	57	71	142
	F-8 Crusader	56	70	141
WSK-Mielec	TS-11 Iskra	24	40	115
Yakovlev	Yak-11	8	24	102
	Yak-18	7	23	101
	Yak-28P	77	88	160